The Heart
of Being Helpful

Peter R. Breggin, MD, is a psychiatrist in private practice in Bethesda, Maryland. He works with children, adults, and families. He is also a forensic medical expert. He is the founder of the Center for the Study of Psychiatry and Psychology and is on the faculty of The Johns Hopkins University Department of Counseling and Human Services. He is noted for his critiques of biological psychiatry and his focus on psychosocial and spiritual alternatives for healing emotional suffering in children and adults.

Dr. Breggin is the author of many books and articles, most recently *Toxic Psychiatry* (1991), *Beyond Conflict* (1992), and with Ginger Ross Breggin, *Talking Back to Prozac* (1994), and *The War Against Children* (1994). *Brain-Disabling Treatments in Psychiatry: Drugs, Electroshock, and the Role of the FDA* will be published by Springer Publishing Company in 1997.

Dr. Breggin's work is frequently covered in the national media, such as the *New York Times, Time, Washington Post, Los Angeles Times, The New Yorker,* the *Chronicle of Higher Education,* and *Science.*

Dr. Breggin and the Center can be visited at their website, www.breggin.com.

The Heart
of Being Helpful

Empathy and the Creation
of a Healing Presence

Peter R. Breggin, MD

 Springer Publishing Company

Springer Publishing Company, Inc.
536 Broadway
New York, NY 10012-3955

Cover photograph by Ginger Ross Breggin.
Cover design by Margaret Dunin.
Acquisition Editor: Bill Tucker
Production Editor: Pamela Lankas

01 02 / 4 3

Library of Congress Cataloging-in-Publication-Data

Breggin, Peter Roger, 1936–
    The heart of being helpful : empathy and the creation of a healing
presence / Peter R. Breggin.
        p.   cm.
    Includes index.

    ISBN 0-8261-9681-0
    1. Empathy.   2. Psychotherapist and patient.   I. Title.
RC489.E46B74   1997
616.89'14—dc21   97-2442
                                                              CIP

*It takes all of our lives to become brave enough
to speak what's in our hearts.*
—Ginger Ross Breggin

Nearly all of us are called upon at one time or another to help
people in emotional and spiritual distress. We do this as friends,
family members, employers, ministers, educators, therapists, and
health professionals. This book is dedicated to those who wish
to respond to others in a spirit of caring and empathy.

Books by Peter R. Breggin, MD

NONFICTION

College Students in a Mental Hospital: An Account of Organized Social Contacts Between College Volunteers and Mental Patients in a Hospital Community (1962) (Jointly authored by Umbarger et al.)

Electroshock: Its Brain-Disabling Effects (1979)

The Psychology of Freedom: Liberty and Love as a Way of Life (1980)

Psychiatric Drugs: Hazards to the Brain (1983)

Toxic Psychiatry: Why Therapy, Empathy, and Love Must Replace the Drugs, Electroshock, and Biochemical Theories of the 'New Psychiatry' (1991)

Beyond Conflict: From Self-Help and Psychotherapy to Peacemaking (1992)

Talking Back to Prozac: What Doctors Aren't Telling You About Today's Most Controversial Drug (1994) (Co-authored by Ginger Breggin)

The War Against Children: The Government's Intrusion Into Schools, Families, and Communities in Search of a Medical "Cure" for Violence (1994) (Co-authored by Ginger Ross Breggin)

Psychosocial Approaches to Deeply Disturbed Persons (1996) (Co-edited by E. Mark Stern)

Brain-Disabling Treatments in Psychiatry: Drugs, Electroshock, and the Role of the FDA (1997)

FICTION

The Crazy from the Sane (1971)

After the Good War (1972)

Contents

Acknowledgments   *ix*

1   Creation of Healing Presence   1

2   Being in Someone Else's Presence   11

3   Acceptance of Our Own Personal Inadequacy   21

4   Nurturing of Human Nature   29

5   Does Empathy Hurt Too Much?   39

6   Does Empathy Make Us Too Vulnerable?   51

7   Beyond the Quick and Easy Cure   61

8   From Fear and Helplessness to Love   71

9   How to Help in Extreme Emotional Crises   83

10 Creation of Healing Aura in Families   95

11 Helping People Who Seem Very Different from Us   109

12 Empathy and the Reform Spirit   121

13 Finding Ourselves Through Principled Living   127

14 Empathy and Forgiveness for Grievous Misdeeds   135

15 Empathy for Children and Childhood   145

16   Importance of Empathy for Ourselves   157

17   Grateful Healer   167

18   Is Love Enough?   175

Index   181

Acknowledgments

I am very much indebted to the many people who have opened their hearts to me over the years. The themes of their lives appear throughout this book. I have, in every instance, however, disguised and reshaped the stories so that they no longer represent one particular person. Because of the universal themes, some individuals might feel that I'm talking specifically about them but in reality I'm drawing on a broader experience than that of any one person.

I especially wish to thank Kevin McCready, Clinical Director of the San Joaquin Psychotherapy Center in Clovis, California, who edited the manuscript and made many worthwhile comments and additions. Nelia Butler was extraordinary in her detailed editing of the final manuscript. Joe Tarantolo and Teresa Dyck made several insightful observations that improved the book. In addition, I received valuable editorial comments and encouragement from David Jacobs, David Cohen, Bertram Karon, Fred Hanna, Rae Unzicker, Eugene Kelly, Jr., Diane Bullock-Johnson, Karen Mittelman, William Bound, Robin Heisler, Jewyll Davis, Sharon Collins, and Leslie Wolowitz. Timothy Falb suggested the term *healing presence*.

Recently I have begun to teach at the Department of Counseling and Human Services of The Johns Hopkins University and I especially want to thank the chairperson, Fred Bemak. I also want to thank George Washington University Professor of Counseling Clemmont Vontress. I'm grateful to Lisbet Larsen and Larry Epp, who introduced me into the counseling community.

My former assistant, Melissa Magruder, remains "like family" to us. I thank her for her specific editorial help and for her overall assistance, which enabled me to find the time to write.

My wife, Ginger, continues to cast her brilliant, loving spirit over my life and work.

Creation of Healing Presence

1

What's wrong with treating emotional crises the way we treat medical emergencies? Why should we transform ourselves in the process of trying to help other people? How can we fine-tune ourselves to the feelings of others?

I was a medical student recently assigned to the Intensive Care Unit (ICU) at the training hospital. Abruptly, warning beeps pierced the ward as a patient went into cardiac arrest. The nurse grabbed a phone and the call went out on the hospital public address system: "Code Blue. ICU."

The nurses quickly checked the man who now lay dead in his bed. His body sprouted various tubes from his nose, mouth, and arm veins, and he looked emaciated. As the nurses began to fuss somewhat aimlessly over him, the Code Blue team rushed in like an assault troop. A large muscular surgeon barked orders and then leaped onto the bed where he began external cardiac massage. He heaved up and down above the patient, pressing rhythmically with the palms of both hands on the sternum of the man's chest. I heard ribs crack beneath the doctor's thrust but the sound did not daunt him or his emergency rescue team.

As we watched, one of the nurses explained to me that the patient had been suffering from end-stage kidney disease and was not expected to live. That's why she chose not to attempt to resuscitate him the instant his heart stopped. After a few minutes, the Code Blue team gave up as well and vanished from the scene almost as rapidly as it had come.

It was my first Code Blue and I would never forget it, especially the sight of the surgeon pressing his weight up and down on the man's chest amid sounds of cracking ribs. As startling as it was, it fit my notion of help—*real* help. Here were doctors doing everything they could, even in a hopeless case.

In medicine there is a concept of "heroic treatment"—radical interventions reserved for extreme cases. Using a penknife for an emergency tracheotomy can fall into that category. In a restaurant, a man has a severe allergic reaction to eating shellfish and goes into laryngospasm. His throat tightens and closes shut, preventing him from moving air in or out of his lungs. As a doctor, you locate the exact spot in the cartilage of his throat where it's safe to penetrate. You slice through cleanly with any available sharp knife, and then insert the barrel of a pen or some other tube to keep the air passage open. That's heroic. It's also potentially disastrous if the doctor overreacts and takes such a drastic action without cause.

Radical cancer surgery and chemotherapy sometimes fall into this category of heroic treatment. In the beginning, so did bone marrow transplantation and kidney dialysis, but they are now considered routine in many cases.

I don't know the origin of the term *heroic treatment*. I'm unsure who the hero is, but presumably it's the doctor who "dares" to go to extremes to save his seemingly "hopeless case." Under these circumstances the patient is often given little or no choice, removing any potential for his or her heroism.

Especially for those of us trained as health care providers, heroic treatment has great appeal. We go to the limit to drag our client from the jaws of death. We pull out all the stops, give it our best shot, and so on. When our client is in an extreme condition, there's little or nothing to lose, we tell ourselves.

In medical school, students are taught to prepare themselves in advance for medical emergencies. You're an intern taking a much-needed nap at 2 A.M. when the emergency room nurse rings you. The ambulance is bringing in a man with chest pain and shortness of breath. As you verbally slap yourself awake, you begin your differential diagnosis in your head. The obvious suspicion is a coronary thrombosis—a heart attack. But it could be something else. (I remember the intern who rushed into a similar situation and administered a dose of morphine for cardiac pain, but the patient turned out to be suffering from an asthma attack—something morphine can worsen.) As you prepare for the emergency as a young medical intern, you coach yourself to think through the differential diagnosis and the acute treatment, even before the patient arrives. You must prepare yourself to act rationally, yet swiftly, when necessary.

Emergency medicine is the model that many professionals use to approach psychological emergencies. It spills over into how many of us in everday life feel we are supposed to respond to friends, family, or others in dire need.

The role of the heroic or authoritarian healer plays into a "culture of helplessness." There is an overall tendency to surrender our physical and spiritual health to "experts." The experts in turn typically have too little time and too little interest in us as individuals to provide treatments that meet our personal needs. This is true in medicine in general, where specialists are likely to focus on a part of our body to the exclusion of our overall health. Recently a friend of mine had a hormonal problem, and had to shuttle from one expert to another, each of whom specialized in one particular hormone. It is even more of a problem in mental health where a specialist in psychopharmacology is likely to summarily reduce the most complex and profound spiritual problems to a biochemical imbalance suitable for correction with drugs. You come for help for an injured psyche, and the doctor treats you for a sick brain, or even more narrowly, for a presumed aberration in a specific biochemical reaction in your brain.

Perhaps more than medicine and surgery in general, psychiatry has had—and continues to have—its heroic treatments. Biological psychiatry continues to display an unrelenting tradition of heroic treatment that impacts negatively on the entire mental health profession, and even on society in general. It encourages people in general to seek quick and dramatic "fixes" (chapter 7).

As a medical expert in malpractice suits, I have testified on behalf of patients who have been subjected to 6, 8, or 10 different psychiatric drugs at once, sometimes against their will. I once testified in a malpractice suit in which a doctor put his patient on 12 psychiatric medications at once. The doctor's colleagues, including the department chairman, knew about his excesses, but did nothing to stop them. When his patients failed to do well, or rebelled against his abusive authoritarianism, this psychiatrist sometimes gave them electroshock or referred them for cingulotomy, a variation of lobotomy.

Restraint is another form of heroic treatment in psychiatry. When unable to develop rapport with our patients or to calm them down with personal contact and reassurance, we strap them into straitjackets, tie them down to chairs, or put them in four-point restraints on a bed. Sometimes we lock them in "rubber rooms" for hours at a time.

Psychiatry doesn't have a monopoly on heroic measures. They are all too common in everyday life. Parents who end up spanking their children—even though they don't believe in spanking—do so because they feel compelled to take extreme measures. Often we feel tempted to "shake some sense" into one of our children and too often we actually try to do it, sometimes resulting in brain injury or death. In dealing with our teenage children, most of us have been tempted to take other extreme stands, such as "grounding" them for months or locking them in their room. Even when we control these impulses, we may joke with our spouse or friends about the things we'd like to do to our children—for their own good, of course.

As surprising as it may seem, men who beat their wives often believe "it's for their own good." Like the doctors who practice heroic therapy, they justify it as a last resort when nothing else seems to help. As one man in couples therapy said to me, "What else could I do in the situation? She wouldn't listen to reason." He looked dumfounded when I asked: "And are you going to hit me when you think I'm not listening to reason?" Our heroic treatments are usually reserved for those who are unable to resist.

The abusive husband is hardly alone in his rationalizations. Many of us have, at the least, yelled angrily in frustration at people we wish to help. There's something in all of us that envisions the necessity of emotionally or even physically coercive help as a last resort. We find ourselves tempted or even compelled to do something drastic to those whom we believe need changing.

There is an occasional place for heroic treatment. If the potential for productive life remained in me, I'd want a surgeon to take heroic measures to revive me from a stroke or heart attack. If I were delirious from an inflammation of the brain, I'd want the hospital staff to restrain me from pulling out the intravenous tubes filled with life-saving antibiotics. I'd want the same done for someone else. But there's too much "heroism" in how most of us generally approach giving help.

From therapy to friendship to family life, doing something drastic or dramatic to the other person is rarely in their best interest. Being genuinely helpful has more to do with a certain way of being than with doing a certain thing. Healing presence does not smack of heroism; it's more like radiating comfort with oneself and others, even under emotional duress.

Too many of the things we do in the name of help are aimed at getting others to conform to our expectations. We want to get their minds and their behaviors in line with our standards for them. We try to do it through several means, including advice, guidance, and direction; new insight and understanding; moral instruction; morale boosting, and the like. In frustration, we can end up trying to argue the other person out of feeling upset. Sometimes, in righteous frustration, we resort to outright force.

The creation of a healing presence focuses on ourselves rather than on the person we are trying to heal or to help. In creating healing presence, we don't change the other person as much as we transform ourselves in response to the other person. We find within ourselves the inner resources that speak directly to the other person's psychological and spiritual needs. This can be stated as the principle of empathic self-transformation:

> To create healing presence, we fine-tune our inner experience to the inner state of the other person. We transform ourselves in response to the basic needs of the person we are trying to heal and to help. Ultimately, we find within ourselves the psychological and spiritual resources required to nourish and to empower the other human being.

Empathic self-transformation may at first seem unrealistic, abstract, or impractical. In reality, it can become a living principle that guides us in all our encounters with people we care about and love. Although it remains basic to all relationships, it becomes especially crucial when we're faced with psychological or spiritual emergencies—extremes of emotional turmoil in which the other person feels hopelessly overwhelmed (chapter 9).

Empathy and the willingness to transform ourselves lie at the heart of being helpful. To help other people, we must be willing to change ourselves to become more responsive to their needs. Empathic self-transformation is the necessary ingredient in creating a healing presence with a client, friend, or family member—with anyone who feels hopeless and beyond help.

Healing presence is a way of being that by its very nature tends to reassure and encourage people, to lend them moral and spiritual strength, to provide confidence that they can overcome suffering and continue to grow. Ultimately, the goal is to help the individual develop his or her own healing presence.

The concept of healing presence has a spiritual aspect. Healing presence is generated by qualities we usually attribute to the soul, being, or self. These attributes include empathy, love, an awareness of values and ideals, and, depending on our views, devotion to humankind and to a higher power.

Healing presence is not magical. It is the product of ways of being in relation to each other. It expresses the reality that the very presence of a person can have a healing effect.

At times I will speak of healing aura—the relationship or the atmosphere created by a healing presence. It is a psychologically and spiritually positive ambience that envelops people or a place.

Some people understandably reject the concept of an aura that invests a relationship or a place. I have accepted it simply because I occasionally experience it, always in a positive manner. The concept does not require a belief in mystical realities. It can be understood as the personal, subjective experience of a positive, joyful, or loving attitude toward other individuals and life.

After reading these pages, Kevin McCready, a Catholic psychologist, reminded me about Christ's declaration, "Where two or more are gathered in my name, there I am." To Kevin, this means that "relationship is essential to spirituality." From my Jewish perspective, Kevin's observation is universal.

Our healing presence helps us to create healing aura with other people. As people learn to join with us in creating this healthy space or aura, they also learn to create the same beneficial conditions with others in their lives.

Aura comes from the Greek word *aura,* meaning breeze or breath of air. It has come to mean any distinctive but intangible emanation or radiation, something subtle, gentle, and invisible. Originally it was used to designate physical emanations, such as the aroma of flowers. Now it is usually reserved for more psychological or spiritual emanations from a person, place, or situation, such as the ambience of a room or the radiance of an individual's personality.

As something that surrounds everyone involved in the experience, healing aura bathes and inspires both the healer and the healed, the therapist and the client, the teacher and the pupil, the parent and the child. Healing aura is a mutual responsibility and a mutual creation. The task of the healer or therapist is to take as much responsibility as possible for its creation with the person being helped. Yet the healer and the client alike must remain aware that healing is a shared process requiring the efforts of everyone involved.

Because it is an environment or an atmosphere, healing aura is beneficial for us as well as for the people we are trying to help. Healing aura is an energy that surrounds and gives energy to everyone involved in the experience.

Charisma shares some qualities with healing presence, but it encourages a model of leaders and followers. Charisma is the ability to inspire followers with devotion and enthusiasm to a cause. It encourages disciples rather than independent persons. It is a way of investing oneself with authority over others rather than vesting others with authority over themselves.

Charisma can be helpful in inspiring people. It may play a useful function, for example, in being an exciting speaker or workshop leader. In groups when we want to hold the attention of others or to sway them to a point of view, charisma plays a role. But a good speaker or workshop leader should remain more interested in empowering the listeners and participants than in leading them down a predetermined path.

Similarly, a therapist's enthusiasm for his own life and for therapy can inspire a client to feel encouragement and hope. Ultimately, however, the therapist's task is to help the clients discover these resources within themselves.

Charisma, at its worst, is the inflated presentation of oneself as a magnificent helping person. It depends on communicating a flawless sense of potency. This masquerade is inherently undermining to our clients, patients, students, or children—to anyone who seeks his or her own independence and empowerment. It suggests that we have qualities that are beyond their reach and that they must depend on us for the accomplishment of their goals. It creates a mythology in which we are the central figure and they are lesser beings.

Unlike charisma, which inspires followers or disciples, healing presence embraces all the people who participate and creates conditions in which people feel nurtured, promoted, and empowered in their own independent growth. Again, unlike charisma, healing aura is not something we generate entirely on our own. It requires us to involve another in our personal experience of ourselves, while involving ourselves in their personal experience of themselves. It is a way of being with another person—a healing awareness and ambience that surrounds the helper and the helped alike.

Healing presence—and the creation of healing aura—is at the heart of being a helpful person. It allows us to be as helpful as we can in almost any circumstance in which people are emotionally distressed or upset. It allows us to promote growth in most situations. It also applies to handling our everyday relationships with people.

This idea of *being in a certain way* as the starting point of helping people has evolved over 30 years of clinical practice. It had become so much a part of my approach that it took me some time to recognize it. Like the proverbial fish in the water, I did not realize that I was swimming in something.

Nor did I realize how little the concept had been articulated by other professionals who try to help people with emotional problems, nor how much it is neglected in the training and practice of therapists. In workshops and talks throughout the United States, Canada, and Europe, I would mention the importance of *how to be with people in therapy,* thinking I would devote limited time to it. Then my audience would latch onto it, not letting me move on to other topics. They would want to hear more about this idea of changing oneself rather than changing the other person.

For many people I've talked with, these ideas touch on something they have already felt intuitively. Many helping people— therapists, physicians, teachers, parents, friends—realize they've been practicing some version of it all along. For them, it has been refreshing, inspiring, and empowering to hear it articulated.

I shouldn't have been so surprised that others find these principles so interesting. Nearly all of the progress I have made in my life as a psychiatrist, therapist, friend, father, or husband has involved learning to take these concepts to a higher level—to find a way of *being,* rather than doing, that meets the psychological, social or spiritual needs of the people I am trying to help.

My psychiatric training pointed me in the opposite direction. When trying to help patients, I was taught to focus on their presumed defects instead of looking, first and foremost, at myself to see what I could offer.

The evolution of my approach has required many years. Its fullblown development actually caught me by surprise. I discovered how far it had developed within me when, for the first time, I found myself spending the whole morning in a workshop talking about it with my audience. Instead of analyzing specific kinds of clients and what they needed, I found myself talking about my own emotional and spiritual attitudes: How I had to find within myself a way to relate with interest, enthusiasm, and empathy to the person whom I was trying to help; how I had to find within myself the psychological and spiritual resources to create a healing presence.

I don't want to suggest that I have reached some "fully evolved state" in which I am always a healing presence in therapy or in other aspects of my life. I am suspicious of people who make such claims for themselves. There is a difference between having standards and believing we have become the standard. Part of healing presence, as I shall confirm throughout this book, is recognizing our own personal limitations.

Healing presence is a journey and a process, not an accomplished fact. It requires patience with ourselves and with other people. Pain and frustration accompany the effort, as they do whenever we fully involve ourselves in life. Healing presence acknowledges that suffering and feelings of hopelessness are a part of living.

Healing presence does not substitute for knowledge that may be needed in the process of helping other people. It does not replace the educational, psychological, or medical background that's sometimes needed, for example, to be a good parent, teacher, doctor, or therapist. If we are medical doctors or lawyers, for example, we need expertise in order to treat or counsel people. But we'll be far more effective if we first attend to the creation of healing aura—an environment that encourages well-being. Similarly, if we're teachers, we will need to know our subject matter and to have practiced our teaching skills. But we'll inspire far more people if we can create our own special kind of presence. If we are psychotherapists, we should know about child development and its effect on adult lifestyles. But we'll risk further demoralizing our clients if we don't first attend to the impact of our own presence.

Healing presence is not a private experience. It cannot be learned in isolation, rather it is learned in our relationships with other people, with animals, and with nature. It's about creating the human conditions that promote healing and growth. Especially, it's about how to help people through our very way of being with them— through the psychological and spiritual atmosphere we create with and for them. Ultimately, healing presence is a way of being with other people in order to create a healing relationship or healing aura.

To develop healing presence, above all else, we must pay attention to the way people respond to us. Instead of being focused on what we have to offer, we must be focused on how others respond to our offering. We must care about the feelings of others as much as we care about our own feelings. We must become willing to fine-tune our souls to the souls of others.

Being in Someone Else's Presence $\mathbf{2}$

How can relating to animals bring out our healing qualities?
What does bird-watching teach us about healing presence?

It was toward evening, 2 hours before sundown over the bay and the inevitable disappearance of the sea birds for another night. In the distance, perhaps 75 yards away, a lone great blue heron was still wading on the edge of the salt marsh, a great flat of mud, completely covered with knee-high blades of thick, tough grass. The bird was standing stock-still, its long neck forming an S curve against the background of the lush green marsh, its heavy, straight beak pointing in expectation at an angle toward the water. Nearly 5 feet in height, the slate-colored monarch of the water's edge was not only tall but slender and elegant.

As if totally comfortable in its world, the heron's every movement was made with purpose. No energy or motion was wasted. It waited, poised above potential prey, until mobilized into one clean, slicing motion to spear a fish from beneath the water. A moment after swallowing its victim, it once again became statuesque. Occasionally it would stalk a few feet through the water with studied steps. If slightly alarmed, it would smoothly turn its head like a periscope on its extended neck, and then return to watchfulness over the water.

The heron was pure grace, except on take-off, when it flapped its wings laboriously during its slow ascent. If alarmed it would utter a single or double "awk" as it made off across the water.

In mimicry of these largest wading birds, I too can stand motionless, endlessly observing them in their slow-motion hunting rituals. The great blue heron is my totem bird—the animal being toward whom my spirit yearns. Why? Certainly not because I'm tall or thin. I'm not. Nor am I graceful or elegant. More like clumsy. And most definitely not prone to silence. Patience can also be a challenge to me. Nor do I always feel wholly at one with my environment. Alongside this big bird, I am like a hyperactive ground hog. I appreciate the bird because it possesses qualities I admire but have not fully acquired.

Sometimes when I'm engaged in helping, I·am like the great blue heron. I am patient. Nothing is wasted; everything is attuned to the task and to the other person. It is not always easy for me to make this transformation of myself.

Bird-watching also teaches us about setting limits or restraints on our own behavior toward others. More exactly, it teaches us the patience, discretion, and adaptability required to observe a sensitive and wary being. We cannot bird-watch on our own terms. We can't arbitrarily decide, "I'll watch birds," and then do it successfully. We have to find the cautious creatures in their own habitat and enter their domain without frightening them off. Sometimes we can remain very still while they come to us, but then we must know where they will be or how to draw them to us. And if we want to observe them up close for any length of time, we must be exactly the way they want us to be—a wholly nonthreatening, unobtrusive presence in their surroundings. For example, they may let us stay within a few feet of their feeder, provided we don't look at them. They're watching us all the time; they don't want us doing the same. Bird-watching may not require healing presence, but it requires something very close to it—a completely safe presence.

Observing nature can also teach lessons about the fallibility of our observations. One early spring morning, I was watching a pair of willets on the shoreline of the salt marsh, a stone's throw away. They are delightful, chattery brown birds, a little smaller than a chicken, with long beaks and longer legs. In the distance I saw the dark silhouette of a bird of prey moving across the sky and, at the same moment, it seemed, the willets began a high-pitched rapid chittering sound that was unfamiliar to me. I thought to myself, "It's an alarm call to warn about the hawk." As seeming proof, the rest of the marsh grew momentarily silent. But the chittering continued after the hawk was out of sight and I saw what it really meant: One willet had jumped upon the back of the other and was standing erect. Then it bobbed its tail into position and began to mate. Afterward, one of them began to fiercely preen and the other took a bath on the water's edge.

When we're dealing with a human psyche, we must approach, if at all, the same way we would approach a skittish bird during mating season: with enormous respect for its privacy. And if we're going to learn about the bird, we must set aside our own assumptions about what's going on and pay enough attention to find out what's really happening. We may notice the hawk in the distance but the birds may have something entirely different on their minds.

Healing or rescuing frightened animals draws on our empathic powers and often requires us to transform ourselves in the process. My wife, Ginger, is fond of nature's most common creatures. Sometimes she becomes their defender. Thus our backyard is host to untold numbers of starlings and sparrows. They compete with the clownish gray squirrels for the largesse she bestows on them. There's little room or opportunity for the more colorful and exotic birds that might come by. So it's no surprise that at the salt marsh, Ginger takes a particular fancy to those commoners among sea birds, the "sea rats"—herring gulls that scavenge up and down the coast and sometimes inland as well.

In their own way, herring gulls are splendid creatures. Depending on age and the season, their colors vary from blotchy brown to sharply contrasting black, gray, and white. A brilliant dab of red on the beak signals mating season. Their sharply hooked bills add an air of both dignity and potential menace. Adaptable as any bird, the herring gull competes with smaller, more intelligent crows on the ground for garbage and with the more agile and dashing laughing gulls for scraps thrown in the air. At sea, they flock like clouds around returning fishing vessels looking for scraps. They will hound ferryboats from the air if people throw them bread.

Sometimes I wonder if herring gulls remember how to secure their food from nature.

One crisp, fall morning, Ginger was feeding a flock of perhaps 100 herring gulls off the upper tier of a dock. Some dove and took bread from her hand, others grabbed it out of the air, some waddled awkwardly along the railing to pick up deposits of crumbs. Others waited more lazily in the water for thrown scraps that the others missed in the air. It was a carnival of sea rats.

Usually these voracious birds hang around until there's nothing left to devour. But on this morning, they seemed to gradually disappear, until only a few remained. Respecting their newfound wariness, we retreated to the back of the deck. As if intrepid spirits facing some unknown danger, a few birds hesitantly alighted to pick at the remaining scraps. Then, with some food still remaining, all the birds disappeared from view.

Not expecting to find anything, Ginger and I meandered out to the railing, and beneath us, on the lower level, we saw why the other birds had fled. A giant gull, as large and as strong as a goose, was stuck between the boards of the dock. One foot had somehow slid through the decking planks, and now the creature could not extricate it. Perhaps the webbed foot had become too swollen to withdraw through the space. However it happened, the bird was caught in a wooden trap, its webbed foot too big to be withdrawn from between the tightly spaced boards. Terrified, it pivoted in circles around the pinned leg as if the appendage had been pulled from its socket or broken.

Ginger asked me to wait on the upper deck while she retrieved a small dish towel from the house. Then, by herself, she slowly descended the stairs to where the creature was exhausting itself with frantic turning efforts. As she approached, Ginger kept talking to the bird in a quiet, reassuring voice, explaining that she meant no harm and had come to help.

As Ginger reached the bird, it markedly calmed down. When the bird did thrust its enormous, hooked beak at her, she did not startle, but reassured the animal that she meant no harm. When the bird grew calm again, she draped the towel over its shoulders and gently held down its wings by wrapping her arm around the bird's back. This put her eye to eye with the bird's dangerous beak.

At first, the gull made abortive stabbing motions with its bill toward Ginger, each time holding back before striking. Once, as if to relieve its frustration, it turned and picked lightly at the towel. Then it turned back toward Ginger, and inches from her face and eyes, it reached out once again as if to peck her. Ginger remained calm and reassuring. Instead of attacking, the bird fastened its beak on the sleeve of Ginger's sweater and gently pulled at the threads. It was doing everything it could to inhibit itself from attacking.

Ginger didn't have enough hands by herself to hold the bird and to extricate its foot. Now she asked me to come down to help. As I slowly descended the stairs, with the bird peering up at me in seeming fearful anticipation, she kept talking to it. She repeated my name and explained that I was going to help.

The gull remained calm and made no attempt to peck me as I stuck my face beneath it to examine where the leg had gone through between the planks. Enduring a frightening and painful procedure, the bird let me pull upward on its stuck leg, until I confirmed that it could not be drawn through the narrow space.

There was only one way to get it free, to slide the bird and its leg along the crack between the boards until we came to the end of the edge of the dock, where it would slide free. Fortunately it was a short distance and there was no trim on the dock to block the leg from sliding out. While I held the stuck leg steady to avoid damaging it—and with no resistance from the bird—Ginger slid the animal along the deck until its leg came free. Then she released the bird with a gentle downward thrust toward the water where it landed, rested for a brief moment, and took off, apparently unharmed.

Afterward, Ginger could barely stand up. It wasn't that her legs were cramped from crouching down; she was emotionally spent. She explained to me that as she approached the bird, she had allowed herself to connect emotionally to the bird's pain and fear until she actually felt its anguish. Feeling herself connected soul to soul with the animal, she could then offer reassurance, calming herself and the bird at once. Afterward, she felt spiritually drained, virtually empty of energy, and she needed to sit down to rest. The bird had flown off with a part of her, and Ginger needed to regenerate.

I cannot fully fathom Ginger's healing presence. More than I am able, she seems to hold nothing back in the presence of injured creatures. She makes herself safe and acceptable to them. Beyond that, she identifies with them with an empathic intensity unknown to most of us. She becomes so open to them that her spirit touches and calms them. She is willing to transform herself to meet the necessities of the situation, becoming enormously patient and opening herself to the animal's suffering.

Rarely have I personally experienced anything as intense as Ginger's response to the bird. Doing psychotherapy more often energizes than depletes me. When Ginger helps *people,* she rarely feels drained. The life-and-death nature of the bird's predicament, the potential for the bird to inflict harm on Ginger, and the enormous effort to communicate across species may have momentarily exhausted her. Ginger was, at any rate, quickly restored. She felt joy about connecting with the bird and rescuing it.

Animals are important in the lives of many people. My clients' experiences with their pets, starting in childhood, frequently become important in therapy. Many of my clients have had more loving experiences with animals than with people. Their relationships with animals can provide them a model for how much love they might someday feel for a human being.

In my practice, when I talk about love with my clients, I will give them my definition of love—"joyful awareness"—and ask them to share with me experiences of joy with people when they were growing up. Usually my clients will assure me that they were loved, and that they loved, within their family; but on questioning, they'll be hard-pressed to come forth with details.

I will ask, "Did your mother smile with delight when you got home from school—as if you were an arriving prince or princess?" Often my question will be answered with anxious laughter. The very idea sounds ridiculous.

"Did anyone ever act as if they were simply delighted that you were alive?", I will inquire. If there are no such positive memories with parents, sometimes there will be moments of shared joy with grandparents or other members of the extended family. "Grandpa was always glad to see me. He was always doing things with me that we enjoyed."

But all too frequently, few if any joyfully loving experiences can be recalled with adults. At some point, I will wonder, "Did you have a pet, perhaps a dog or cat?"

"Oh, my dog Freckles, he loved me. Yes, when I'd get home, he'd greet me like I was a prince. I can still see him jumping up on me, trying to lick my face, his tail wagging with all its might."

That *is* love—a joyful awareness, communicated without ambivalence by a dog to a young child. It may be the main reason so many American households have a dog. For human beings, dogs are often the only or the main source of unconditional love. As children, we often learn to love through our pets.

Love is joyful, but it can result in profound sorrow. Like the loss of life itself, the threat of losing love can be utterly demoralizing and even paralyzing. The depth of that sorrow provides a window into the depth of our connectedness to others.

One of my clients, Leanne, was a proper, brittle-looking woman in her forties who had immigrated from Great Britain many years earlier. From her speech to her attire, everything was quite proper. She was in an equally proper relationship, so much so that her fiancé, with whom she would not have sex, was considering an end to their engagement. She talked abstractly about their shared interests, both financial and emotional, and how they matched or didn't match. I got little sense of how she actually felt about him. I also wondered why she seemed so appreciative of me and my therapy with her; we seemed so very different, and I had difficulty feeling warmly toward her.

For many years, Leanne's fiancé had been entirely devoted to her, constant despite her indecision and restraint, and eager to marry her. Now his loneliness and frustration had won out; he needed to start dating other women. She was convinced he would soon be having sex with other women and then she would stop having anything to do with him.

Leanne had written her fiancé a four-page, outraged letter about his supposed betrayal of her, but on advice from me on the telephone, she hadn't as yet mailed it. As I read the letter in our next session together, I tried to figure out how to communicate to her that the problem did not consist of his betrayal of her, but of her inability to make a decision about him. Buried in one of the angry paragraphs was a sentence that read, "Even my cat betrayed me 10 years ago."

I stopped and let the letter fall into my lap. "A cat? I don't think you ever mentioned that to me. I didn't think you liked animals."

She started to cry, dabbing her tears as properly as possible with a tissue. In a few crisp sentences she described how she had owned and loved her cat for five years. From the description of the animal, it had more the personality of a spaniel than a typical feline. Then out of economic necessity, she had taken in a boarder, and the cat, apparently out of "spite," had disappeared—never to return.

"I was so despondent," she said amid tears, "that I lost 15 pounds. My friends feared that I had cancer. I felt so betrayed, I vowed never to own another animal for the rest of my life." That was a decade ago.

When she finished crying, she looked at me with the only truly vulnerable look I'd ever seen on her face. She explained, "There must be something terribly wrong inside my head to suffer over a cat."

"Oh, no," I said from my heart. "Just the opposite. It shows the depth of your soul—your capacity and willingness to love. No wonder you're so afraid to make a decision about your fiancé."

"I told my cat I loved her," she cried again. "I would hold her in my arms before I went to sleep. Every evening. And I would tell her that I loved her."

I reassured Leanne that she need not feel any embarrassment about sharing her experience with me. "Leanne, this is the closest I have ever felt to you. Until this moment, I was puzzled about why you seemed so much to want to work with me. But now I understand. There's so much feeling inside. You've been hiding it from all of us: me, your fiancé . . ."

"And myself. . . ." she finished the sentence for me.

Perhaps for the first time, I felt fully present for Leanne, and she seemed fully present for me.

Leanne and I went on to talk about how lonely she had been all of her life, from childhood until this very moment. The cat had been the one oasis in her emotional desert. Then Leanne began for the first time to talk about how much she loved her fiancé. But if she'd been so hurt by her cat's betrayal of her, how could she survive the impending betrayal by her fiancé?

It was no longer so difficult for Leanne to understand that, if anything, her fiancé's devotion had withstood the test of time. He demonstrated his willingness to love her through years of a seemingly endless, often unfulfilled, engagement. It was time for her to find the courage to make a decision. With no doubt in her mind that she loved him, she decided to scrap the letter in favor of asking her fiancé to marry her. As she made the decision, she had the look of someone filled with love. She radiated joy.

Relating to animals, especially wild birds, can bring out the gentleness and patience required of anyone who wishes to help others with psychological or spiritual problems. Birding, like psychotherapy, requires an exquisite sensitivity to other beings and a willingness to participate in their world on their terms. This is the essence of creating an empathic environment attuned to the needs of those we seek to help.

Acceptance of Our Own Personal Inadequacy

3

Why should we accept our own inadequacies? How does this acceptance allow us to be more helpful to other people?

During my training, one of my therapy supervisors explained that a psychiatrist should always make direct and unequivocal statements. Interpretations, he said, should be spoken with brevity and firmness, more like truths than like opinions. Some of the famous therapists I watched in person or on film took even more aggressive approaches to their clients, a kind of verbal shock treatment.

These styles do more to empower the helper than the helped. It's easy for clients to feel awed by their therapists, when what they really need is to feel more impressed with themselves.

One of my associates, Malcolm, is respected as a well-trained therapist. Until recently, however, I would have been reluctant to go to him for help as a friend or client. I have also wondered if there wasn't something at least a little amiss in how he related to his clients.

Then one day Malcolm told me this story.

"I've always wanted to believe in rationality—in our ultimate ability to control our emotions. It was a subtle thing with me," he explained. "As a therapist, of course I know that people suffer from emotional reactions, obsessions, compulsions, and the like that they cannot control. But I harbored a lingering doubt, a suspicion about the strength of their will power or their resolve when they let their lives be dominated by so much irrationality."

Malcolm took a breath and checked my facial expression before confessing any further. I told him, "I've always struggled with that myself. I no longer even like some of my early writing. It placed too much emphasis on willpower. I was trying too hard to be invulnerable."

"Yes," Malcolm said with relief, "That's just what I'm getting at. It came to me when this thing happened to me at my friend's apartment last weekend. It's a high-rise, 15 stories up, with a balcony jutting out."

Again, Malcolm waited, wanting to see if I was going to judge him. "I remember," I reminded him, "that you .once told me you have a little fear of heights."

"Yes, precisely, a little fear of heights. Nothing much, just a little fear," Malcolm mocked himself. "I was visiting my friend with his wife in their apartment when we got into this terrible argument. His wife thought I'd been disrespectful toward her feelings as a woman. Something stupid I'd said about feminism. He got angry at me for offending her. The whole thing upset me, seemed to get out of control, and I said I needed a break. The only place to get away was on the balcony of their condo."

"Yes?"

"I went outside and stood there looking out over the city and this impulse came over me in a rush. I felt driven to hurl myself off—right off the damn balcony. I felt commanded to do it. In a panic, I wanted to escape the balcony but my friend had closed the sliding door behind me. I was sure he had locked me out—a fatal joke on me. I grabbed and started yanking on the door handle . . . and he saw me . . . and came running across the living room. It wasn't locked. I was fumbling so badly in my fright that I couldn't get it open. I fled back into the apartment, sat down, and shook on the couch."

Malcolm let himself cry.

"Like that, the argument didn't matter anymore. They both sat beside me and hugged me. They hugged me even though they hadn't the slightest idea what was making me behave so crazy."

He was quiet for a minute or so.

"What do you make out of that?" he asked me.

It took me only a minute to share with him a related experience of my own about being overcome with irrational fear.

"Really?" he said.

"Yes," I explained. "You can end up feeling totally out of control. Or worse, under the control of some alien impulse."

"But you know, Peter, a lot of good came from it."

"I'm glad."

"For one thing," Malcolm went on, "I got to the bottom of it. Family conflict of course: my mother angry at me, then my father threatening to kill me. The memory made me so frightened, I thought I'd have to throw myself off the balcony."

Malcolm's mouth was so dry that his tongue was sticking. I brought him a glass of water.

"Peter, something more important came out of it. That panic on the balcony made me feel differently about my clients. Of course, I've always tried to be understanding with them, but now it's different—I *am* understanding with them. I realize how vulnerable they are. I'm a therapist, I have the tools to figure out what's going on inside me, and yet I can still get so frightened. So what about people who aren't trained the way we are? What happens to them when—wham, out of the blue!—wham, they get overcome by something totally irrational and terrifying? It must be even more awful than it was for me."

I nodded my agreement.

"I've got a new feeling about my clients," he told me, "Especially the ones who used to make me impatient. I realize now that their feelings of being out of control are absolutely real to them. For some, their entire lives feel that way, the way I felt on the balcony: driven to throw myself off, with retreat closed off behind me. No wonder they need so much reassurance and support."

I felt for the first time in our relationship that I could trust him if I ever needed to seek help from him. He'd understand.

Another friend, Barry, is also a therapist, and he has understood these issues for a long time. I was having lunch with him when we began discussing yet another colleague.

"The difficulty I have with him," Barry explained, "is that he tries to be adequate to everything." "I'm more comfortable," Barry went on to explain, "with people who let you know they don't feel adequate to everything."

Barry's observation, "He tries to be adequate to everything," was an interesting use of words. Barry was talking about something very subtle. He was saying that the mere pretense of unfailing adequacy was threatening.

I thought about what Barry was saying and realized it was true of my closest friends. They carry themselves with a respect for their own inadequacies, as well as mine.

Should a helping person communicate *in*adequacy?

I remember the news coverage following the bombing of the government building in Oklahoma City. Nearly everyone in America heard about the rescue workers trying to save the injured who were trapped under tons of concrete debris. All of us marveled at the courage of those involved when a decision was made and accepted to amputate a woman's leg to free her from the concrete slab that had pinned her down.

At a moment like that, what would have happened if the doctors and the other members of the rescue team had communicated inadequacy? The mere hint of inadequacy to the task, at least at the critical moments leading up to the emergency surgery, might have created panic in the patient and in the other team members.

So the effort to project complete adequacy probably has a useful function in extreme physical emergencies, competitive sports, military combat, and the boardroom. More exactly, the display of adequacy has a valuable function in *some* aspects of those activities requiring steel nerves: intense concentration and rapid life and death decision-making; and technical or physical prowess under duress. But is this the right model for helping people with emotional problems—even with emotional emergencies or crises? Is it the right model for a parent or teacher when trying to help vulnerable beings to reach their psychological and spiritual potential?

Should the surgeon *always* act as if he is adequate to any task, for example, when he's telling patients that they have incurable cancer? The pretense of adequacy is likely to shut down the surgeon's own humanity and hence his or her capacity to relate to these patients in a supportive, caring fashion. Acting wholly adequate works in some situations and not in others.

What's wrong with communicating unflagging adequacy?

For one thing, it's a pretense. In reality, no one is adequate to every challenge. Some people fold under one kind of pressure, others under another; but everyone has weaknesses and vulnerabilities. Falsifying confidence and competence can get in the way of genuine, intimate, and personally meaningful relationships.

There are some situations in which few of us feel wholly adequate, for example, in facing our own death or the death of others we care about. There are situations that overwhelm some of us but not others, from speaking in public to taking tests, from facing up to a bully to taking on our boss concerning a raise. The surgeon who is unperturbed by physical suffering in his or her patients may be unable to handle emotional pain. Other people may handle emotional suffering much more easily than physical pain.

Some of us quake at dealing with emotional violence, some at dealing with physical violence. Some of us can handle our own sexual impulses but not our violent ones. Some of us can be very tender without growing too afraid, others cannot. The variety of "inadequacies" that we have is infinite.

As helping persons, if we *think* we are adequate to any task, situation, or person, then we are misleading ourselves and may possibly cause harm to others. As a therapist, if we're frightened by a situation or client—and don't admit it to ourselves—we're likely to behave with the sensitivity of a steamroller. The same is true as a minister, teacher, parent, or friend.

Our inevitable inadequacy as individuals is one of the reasons why it's so difficult to function as a single parent. Our children so easily upset and confound us, we need often a partner to provide balance to our reactions when they become too extreme. Some parents "lose it" when a child seems disobedient to their faces. Other parents handle that kind of direct encounter with ease, but can't stand it when their child disobeys them behind their backs. Each parent has something to learn from the other about how to handle stressful situations. One parent can provide help in dealing with direct confrontation; the other can explain how devious behavior can also be dealt with without succumbing to outrage.

Our inevitable inadequacy makes it essential for helping professionals to have adequate resources for consultations with or referrals to other professionals. One therapist may find working with a particular client especially difficult, while another therapist might find it relatively easy.

It's crucial for every therapist to realize that he or she may not be the best person for any given client at any given time. If particular clients don't respond well to us, it may have more to do with us than with them. This is one more reason not to resort to heroic treatments, such as manipulative therapies, drugs, or electroshock. Clients often need a different therapist rather than a more extreme treatment.

The same is true for every kind of helping or service role, from doctors to lawyers, from parents and teachers to friends. The height of wisdom is to recognize that we are not always the best resource for someone else, including our own children, our husband or wife, or our friends.

Being helpful—creating a healing aura—requires enormous respectfulness and sensitivity to our own vulnerabilities, and also to those of others. We must be willing to sense another person's feelings of inadequacy and to be respectful about them. That's a difficult task, if not an impossible one, when we're pretending to ourselves to be unfailingly adequate and invulnerable.

To maintain the myth of our own adequacy, we are likely to reject, deny, or judge other people who communicate their sense of inadequacy to us. We will lack patience and understanding in the face of all those many manifestations of inadequacy that people bring to us when they're asking for help.

If people in emotional trouble are taken in by our masquerade of adequacy, they are likely to feel humiliated in comparison and to feel even more inadequate than before. By coming on as if they can handle anything and anyone, helping persons can end up making those in need feel worse.

When people seek help, especially from professionals, they tend to idealize them—to imagine them as possessing qualities that transcend the human scale. It becomes easy for a therapist or other professional to turn to manipulation and charisma—to try to help by virtue of a seemingly special or superior station in life. But worship of a therapist, teacher, or parent is not ultimately helpful. Any one person's wisdom, ethics, or experience may be more or less adequate compared to another person's, but our fundamental selves are little different. My needs are the same as yours; and when they are thwarted, I suffer in the same fashion as you. This is true for all of us. To be helpful, we should not disguise this truth: we should emphasize it. It is to the glory—and sometimes the ignominy—of us all that we are members of the same species.

To create a truly therapeutic aura, we must communicate a realistic, honest sense of our level of adequacy in various situations. If we do feel completely comfortable with another person and able to be fully present in dealing with his or her emotional crisis, then we can let ourselves feel and express it. For example, if a client talks about being suicidal, we might feel confident in handling it, and that confidence can be communicated. But if the threat of suicide frightens us, as it should if it seems a real possibility, it's better to let the person know our feelings. Most important, we should not try to carry ourselves as if we're adequate to anything and everything. Faking undermines healing presence. An acceptance of our limits contributes positively to a healing aura, making us more comfortable with ourselves and allowing others to face their vulnerabilities without shame.

Nurturing of Human Nature

4

What are basic human needs? How should we respond to the needs of other people? Why should we take care of our own needs before trying to be helpful? Why is it important to place strict limits on the kinds of satisfactions provided in helping relationships?

Armand is a profoundly thoughtful man who goes through daily spasms of resentment and distrust toward the whole of humankind. At these times, Armand looks at the world and sees nothing but hate, greed, and manipulation. He piles newspaper clippings around his desk to remind himself of the human condition. If a visitor to his office challenges his cynicism, he picks a clipping at random from the piles and hands it to his guest.

When Armand's wife professes love for him—when she acts on impulses of love—he often fears manipulation and withdraws from her. Knowing about Armand's childhood, it's easy to understand how he became an expert on perceiving the dark side of life. Neither parent unconditionally loved him, and his father regularly humiliated him. The one teacher who seemed to care about him tried to sexually molest him; the teacher later was arrested and imprisoned. That's when Armand first began to collect newspaper clippings.

Despite Armand's fears of being manipulated by his wife, he was in reality manipulating her. He did things to push her away, to discourage her, to make her feel less confident—all to fend off her love. Even when he felt loving toward her, he was likely to hold back for fear of giving her an advantage in their conflicts. When I pointed out these manipulations to him, he readily agreed. He was painfully honest with himself.

I told Armand that I agreed with him about the sad state of the human condition. I said to him, "There's love—and then there is everything else." I added, "the abuse, hate, and violence is the everything else."

Anyone who looks clearly at society will see human beings competing to gain advantage over one another, human beings using and manipulating each other, human beings torturing and killing each other. Except where there is love, there are all those other things—the "everything else" so dreadfully characteristic of human life.

Where there is love, we make another's well-being as important and sometimes even more important than our own. We glory in another's success, satisfaction, and happiness as much or more than we would in our own. Love, remember, is a "joyful awareness" that inspires caring, nurturing, and treasuring.

A friend of mine met a woman while traveling on a train in a foreign country. She was from another culture, and he anticipated they would never see each other again. They cried together as they talked about their past love lives, and their hopes and aspirations for the future. Nothing like this had ever happened to him before.

Five years earlier, the woman explained, her husband had died. The recollection of their years together continued to make her glow as a woman newly in love.

My friend said to her, "You shared that with someone for 20 years? I haven't had it for 2 hours."

He laughed self-consciously and looked at his watch, realizing he was referring to his brief time with her. His 2 hours with her, with this stranger, were more intimate and caring than anything he could remember. His encounter with this stranger left him inspired to seek more for himself in his relationships.

When he told me the story, I said to him, "Everything good flows from that—flows from love."

"We were, weren't we—we were loving each other?"

"In love with each other and in love with life," I added.

Everything good flows from love. Everything good is an expression of joyful awareness. Our dedication to social justice or the environment is best inspired by love for people and nature. Even a sense of profound tragedy depends on our awareness of what life potentially can offer.

A healing presence communicates love; it addresses the need to love and be loved. Through the creation of a loving aura, healing presence encourages the resolution of hateful inner conflicts within the other person.

Love can be called a basic need—a capacity or potential that yearns for fulfillment in every infant, child, and adult.

Love may be *the* basic need—the one that underpins and sheds light on all the others. We need to be joyfully aware of each other, to nurture and to care for each other, to treasure each other. We need to love ourselves and other people, and we need to love much of what we do in life. We need to love the human community and life itself.

Love can be abused, perverted, denied, and buried beneath stony defenses. But it remains smoldering like lava at our core. Love is the heat of life.

Humanistic and existential psychologists have sought to find one central or guiding impulse of human life. They have called it self-realization, self-actualization, and individuation. If there is such a central principle, we could also call it love—love for ourselves, for others, and for life. As we begin to tease out one or another need, we find a greater, richer, and more varied fabric—an overall need to live more fully or to be in love with life.

We learn about love and other needs by looking into our hearts and minds. In this sense, all psychology is autobiography. At the least, psychology begins as autobiography, and then becomes informed and refined through our awareness of the lives of others. Only if we can identify these human needs within ourselves can we recognize and address them in others.

The basic or universal needs are psychological, social, and spiritual.[1] Physical needs also affect us, such as hunger, sex, and the

---

[1] For a detailed discussion of basic needs, including citations to other authors, see my book, *Beyond Conflict* (1992).

relief of pain. Physical needs can energize us, but they cannot direct how we will react to them. For example, people who are starving rarely kill their neighbors over food. Poor people who need basic shelter do not commonly steal or invade other people's homes. People who are sexually frustrated don't ordinarily commit rape. Even in the face of painfully frustrated biological needs, the individual's actions will be determined, for better or worse, by personal and cultural values.

There are many alternative ways to list or to describe the array of basic needs. There are needs for love and esteem; for emotional safety and security; for relief from extremely painful emotions such as guilt, shame, and anxiety; for autonomy and independence; for recognition of one's identity, individuality, or unique self; for authenticity, genuineness, sincerity, or honesty in our relationships; for the exercise of our cognitive, creative, and spiritual capacities; for the performance of useful and worthwhile activities; for purpose in our lives; for knowledge of our place in the past, present, and future history of our family, culture, and planet; for meaning beyond ourselves through family, country, humanity, nature, or a higher power.

Many of the basic needs are expressions of love. Love can be viewed as the fundamental social need. A person who does not love is a person who is barely alive.

For the infant, being loved provides the spiritual sustenance necessary for normal psychological and social development. In the process of feeding and holding the infant, love becomes inseparable from physical warmth, from being fed, and from feeling physically safe and secure.

As the child grows toward adulthood, the need to be loving becomes as important as being loved. We thrive on loving family and friends, art and creativity, worthwhile work, life-affirming secular or religious principles, humankind, and nature.

Very early in life, some subtle basic needs become apparent. Children, for example, are very aware of their needs for authenticity, for respect, and for love. Often they can sense an adult who is "phony" or who doesn't give them genuine respect or love. Frequently, they do this more readily than adults, who have blunted their perceptions while accommodating unhappiness and frustration.

We need love and we desire to give love. We need esteem and we desire to esteem others. Even in physical pain, we not only need relief from our own suffering, we want to avoid inflicting our pain on others. Every need can be understood as a dynamic interaction between people, an active giving and receiving, rather than as an impulse experienced by an isolated person.

The need for esteem, love, or identity cannot be separated from the people who promote or injure our esteem, who share or reject our love, who enhance or threaten our identity. Satisfactions gained through nature or art also will depend for their meaning on our social and cultural background and experiences. As an example of how culture affects our way of viewing nature, I remember the words of a Native American who explained to European settlers, "We don't call the woods a wilderness." The Native American was grateful for the woods that provided him his sustenance, his home, and his spiritual center.

We should be cautious about making a formal, complete list of basic human needs. We are subtle and complex beings that defy simplification and dissection. Each of us should be approached as a fresh, unique expression of commonly shared human needs.

Notice that relief from painful emotions is but one among many basic needs. We should not focus exclusively on the relief of distress rather than on understanding the underlying sources of pain. Emotional pain is a part of life. Often, severe emotional suffering goes with the human territory.

Even within physical medicine, it can be hazardous to provide pain relief without dealing with the underlying disorder. As physicians, we avoid giving too much analgesia to a patient with an acute head injury because it can mask the source and the severity of the underlying problem. In addition, the analgesic medication can further impair the function of the injured brain.

In the arena of emotional problems, it is even more important to avoid suppressing pain. Attempts to suppress painful feelings can do more harm than good. These attempts give the wrong impression to clients—that their suffering is the problem, rather than a signal of their problems. Intense emotions should be viewed as indicators that something important is going on rather than as symptoms to be eradicated.

Some psychologists have suggested that needs occur in hierarchies, so that survival needs take first priority. In real life, however, people frequently put values and ideals ahead of food, shelter, or physical safety. Commonly, people live and die on the basis of their beliefs. People frequently commit suicide rather than act in ways that offend their beliefs. More positively, a woman who is starving is likely to feed her children ahead of herself. A man or woman may set aside personal aspirations to earn money for the family.

We do not live by bread alone; often, we do not put bread ahead of our ethics or values—our more social or spiritual needs. All cultures have real or mythic heroes who put wisdom, courage, and other ideals ahead of creature comfort or survival.

Basic needs lie at the heart of human nature itself. The fulfillment of these needs is the fulfillment of ourselves as human beings—what has been called "becoming fully human." All cultures and societies recognize that human beings need a great deal more than the satisfaction of their survival needs.

Bonding is both an expression of love and a method for satisfying a broad array of human needs. Bonding is a mutual relationship in which people assign great importance and meaning to each other. When people bond, they form a loving partnership to meet each other's basic needs.

Sometimes people act or talk as if they reject some of their basic needs, including bonding. Instead of pursuing love, they withdraw into relative isolation. Instead of seeking autonomy and independence, they ask or even demand to be treated as helpless children in need of authoritarian instruction and control.

Sometimes psychiatrists use helpless behavior to justify taking charge of the individual's life. Catering to helplessness always disempowers a person. There are much better ways to obtain security, including the development of one's own abilities and independence (chapter 8).

If so many people display a desire to give up their autonomy, should we call helplessness a basic need? Because there is so much violence in the world, should we call aggression a basic need, too? Or should we conclude that these destructive reactions result from the thwarting of more basic, healthy needs?

These are in part semantic questions. How should we label human desires or responses that obviously cause harm? There are also real issues here about the origin of negative impulses such as helplessness and violence. Some people believe that these apparent needs spring from frustration and suffering. Others believe that these needs are a genetic part of human nature.

Whether destructive impulses are built into us or not, all people are sometimes motivated or driven in directions that are harmful to themselves and to others. Even with a relatively good upbringing in a more ideal society, many people would probably continue to struggle with self-defeating or destructive feelings. However, in this book I'm reserving the term *basic needs* for positive expressions of human nature.

All helping relationships address passionate, universal needs. This makes for potentially volatile, out-of-control ways of relating. For this reason, helping relationships require carefully preserved limits.

Therapists, family members, ministers, teachers, coaches—all must approach "being helpful" with great care not to take advantage. They also need to learn to prevent clients and other people from taking advantage of them. Before trying to develop healing presence, a person should have a good grasp of the ethical restraints required in being a parent, teacher, minister, or therapist. Otherwise, temptation can overcome ethical and professional considerations.

Parents, for example, may be tempted to turn to their children for satisfactions that lie outside the legitimate parent–child relationship. Instead of turning to other adults, they may use their children for intimacy and security. This makes children feel guilty about growing up and leaving their parents. In the extreme, parents can cause great harm by using their children sexually or as objects upon whom to vent their frustrations. Parenting, like conducting therapy, often requires self-restraint.

When parents make a child too important to their own social satisfactions, the child may have trouble growing up and leaving home. For the complete fulfillment of our needs as adults, we must turn to other adults outside the context of parenting.

Persons who offer services and help to vulnerable people must accept limits on their own personal gratification, especially their gratification for intimacy. Intimacy in its full expression should be reserved for relationships between equals, not for helping relationships in which one individual possesses more authority, influence, or control than the other.

The purpose of therapy, and many other professional relationships, is not to provide a lifelong, satisfying partnership, but to help the client or student to become more independent. Expressions of love within therapy should always be made within the context of recognizing the limits of therapy as a place for fulfilling these needs. The therapist should never relate to a client as someone who fulfills the therapist's needs for love. Social contacts, even after the termination of therapy, should usually be avoided. Sexual contacts should always be forbidden.

Maintaining limits on the therapist–client relationship is an inherent part of why therapy works. People often come to therapy because they have been unable to have their needs met without professional help. They require a carefully controlled setting in which they can safely explore their feelings and conflicts about themselves and other people. This cannot be done if the therapy becomes one more threatening personal relationship.

If we are going to devote ourselves to helping others, we need to feel relatively satisfied in our own personal lives. This reduces the temptation to step beyond the proper limits of any kind of professional relationship, such as teaching or therapy. Having a satisfying life also helps parents avoid relying too much on their children.

Therapists and parents are human, however, with all the frailties inherent in that condition. During our lives we will undergo our own losses and disappointments, even our own tragedies and catastrophes. This is all the more reason to set careful limits on how we relate to the vulnerable people in our lives, including clients, students, and children.

Being a helping person starts with taking care of oneself. If we take care of ourselves in the presence of other beings, we are much more likely to take care of them as well. This is not a mere metaphor; it has consequences for us and those we care about. As psychologist Kevin McCready reminded me, in its emergency instructions, every airline informs its adult passengers to put on their own oxygen mask before trying to assist others, including children.

Establishing a safe setting for oneself is as necessary for informal helping relationships as for formal therapy. If you are going to listen to a friend's troubles, you need to feel that you're emotionally prepared to pay attention, that you have sufficient unhurried time, that too much isn't being asked of you, that you're not being drawn against your wishes into conflicts with other friends, that you care enough to want to help, that helping seems basically enjoyable or fulfilling for you, and that your friend isn't coercing you with dire outcomes, such as "You've got to help or I'll kill myself."

In trying to help others, the first person we should "diagnose" is ourself—how we are relating to our own needs and to the needs of the other person, and especially whether we are as caring and empathic as we can be toward ourselves and the other person. One purpose of creating the safe environment is to maximize our potential for empathic relating, the essence of healing presence.

While placing limits on the mutual satisfactions provided in helping relationships, we must not reduce the interchange to one direction only. In creating healing presence, we must recognize that the other person—the person we are helping—has the need to give to us as well. Most helping relationships become bonding experiences. If the relationship is unidirectional—if we envision ourselves as giving without receiving anything in return—we create a relationship that demeans the other person and thwarts his or her basic needs. We fail to create healing aura.

When we try to help others, we must be sensitive to how they experience their own needs. The persons being helped may be so terrified of love, or so cynical about it, that we cannot directly address or speak about love with them. As children, their parents may have told them "I love you" when justifying unfair punishments and deprivations. As adults, their husbands or wives may have declared "I love you" when they were acting hatefully. We may have to signal fondness or affection in subtle, nonthreatening ways, such as by our courtesy, kindness, and persistent attentiveness to their feelings and experiences.

In general, we cannot create the conditions for meeting other people's needs only by talking about these needs. We create a healing environment by being helpers who radiate love, respect, or caring and who accept these expressions from others.

Many people have been so injured by the religious experiences imposed on them in childhood that they associate "spiritual values" with coerced self-sacrifice and guilt. When they wish for more spiritual satisfaction, we can help them to distinguish between their own unfortunate experiences and the enormous potential for spiritual satisfaction offered by many different approaches.

People vary widely in how they seek to satisfy their most fundamental needs for love and for bonding. Some pursue romantic love as the most satisfying life experience. Others find joy through God and seek a monastic life. Some people pour themselves into work and other creative activities that bring them enormous satisfaction. As helpers, we must develop a deep appreciation for the varied ways in which people go about living satisfying lives.

Becoming as empathic as possible is not the only principle at work in helping people, but it is the primary one, the sine qua non. Empathy is the necessary condition for helping others.

As a psychiatrist and a therapist, I do a great deal more than create a healing presence. I draw upon specific knowledge and skills, as well as lessons learned from life and from years of doing therapy. Some of the techniques of therapy will be described in this book. None of them are very useful without an underlying healing presence.

Before a setting can become therapeutic, before a relationship can become genuinely helpful, and before any useful communication can take place, change usually has to begin within the helper. The helper must empathize with himself or herself and with the other person to create a safe, encouraging environment. Basking in that healing aura, both individuals can have the opportunity to continue communicating, learning, and growing with each other.

Does Empathy Hurt Too Much?

5

Can we become too empathic—too sensitive and easily hurt? How can we remain aware of suffering without being overwhelmed by it?

The philosophic question is often bandied about, "If a tree falls in the forest where no one can hear it, does it make a sound?" For many people, the real question seems to be "If a tree falls on someone else, has it fallen at all?"

For some people, starting as children, empathy springs forth as naturally as from a fountain. When one of my daughters was barely old enough to toddle with me hand-in-hand around the block, I stopped with her in front of a telephone pole and explained that it was made from the trunk of a tree. With a worried look on her face, she asked "But where did the tree go?" Failing to recognize the spiritual depth of her question, I spent minutes patiently explaining about branches and firewood, bark and mulch, leaves and compost. She kept repeating, "Where did the tree go?" until I realized she was concerned for the fate of its spirit or soul. In retrospect, I wish I had been more aware of my own deep feelings about nature and trees. Later I would take great joy in caring for trees and in watching them grow. But in regard to that, I was a toddler at the time.

Being an enlightened child can result in special problems. A lively child, Angela radiated "something different" from the rest of her family. Sometimes her mother compared her to a free spirit from a fairy tale. At other times she seemed "too sensitive"—the kind of child that seemed to have been born with a caring heart. Her mom nicknamed her "the sad little angel."

While there was some recognition in the family of Angela's special qualities, there was never wholehearted acceptance. She always felt different, especially from her father and her brothers. They teased her for crying too easily. They made fun of the way she seemed at times to "carry the weight of the world on her shoulders." They did not stop to wonder why such a lively spirit seemed so sad at times.

As a grown woman, Angela by nature seemed bursting with energy and enthusiasm for life. Everywhere she went, often with hardly a moment's introduction, she could make friends and engage people in meaningful encounters. She did it forthrightly and without pretense at work, in her circle of friends, and sometimes simply bumping into strangers.

After a series of tragic losses among her friends, some of whom died of AIDS, Angela found it hard to recuperate. She grew depressed and began to wonder if she ever plumbed the depths of the people she knew. She began to think again about herself as the sad little angel. The childhood persona symbolized the confusions and contradictions in herself and her life—the lighthearted child with the heavy heart, the grown woman whose spirit yearned for freedom and yet withdrew in sadness from the suffering she saw around her. She read an early manuscript version of this chapter and it helped to revitalize her spirit; but before listening to her insights and responses, let's continue with the substance of the chapter.

Erich, like Angela, couldn't stand to be aware of other people's suffering. He often had difficulty noticing what his wife was feeling, especially if she was in emotional pain. When he recognized that she was suffering, he then found it hard to respond in a nurturing manner. Before couples therapy, he often withdrew when she needed him.

During one session Erich remarked that every time he heard or read about human rights violations around the world it made him feel sick. Sometimes he couldn't read the newspaper because it was so physically upsetting to him. It turned out that any kind of human suffering seemed unendurable to him, whether it emanated from strangers or from his own wife.

Erich's reactions frustrated and compromised him because he had a lifelong interest in injustice and in the amelioration of human suffering. He also cared a great deal about his wife and wished he could be in touch with her more painful feelings.

Erich had obtained a graduate degree in the social sciences in part because of these concerns about other people and humanity, but never pursued a career in the field. Instead, as an extremely bright young man, he had drifted into computer programming because it was easy, made money, and allowed him to be isolated. Meanwhile, he felt shut down professionally.

Erich believed that he withdrew from suffering because he had "too much empathy, too much sensitivity." There was an important kernel of truth in this, but it missed the critical point. While he was more aware of injustice and suffering than most people, his responses were not empathic. His responses did not motivate him to focus on the people who were suffering. They did not encourage him to learn more about them or to want to try to help them. Instead, his reactions turned inward on himself, focusing him on his own emotional paralysis and feelings of impotence. Sometimes he would actually grow physically weak and experience a sick feeling in his own stomach. Rather than reacting to the suffering of others, he was in reality reacting to unendurable pain inside himself that was stirred up by suffering he perceived in others.

As his wife confirmed in the sessions, Erich was far and away the most sensitive and aware person in his entire family. The rest of the family seemed either singularly lacking in awareness or so injured that they could not let it surface. Growing up in this family, Erich had to grapple alone with his potentially empathic awareness, and he'd become overwhelmed by his feelings.

In Erich's family, suffering of any kind was shoved under the rug. No one talked about "those things," whether it involved family members or people elsewhere in the world. The family members didn't feel capable of dealing with the human condition, so they made believe it didn't exist.

Erich knew there was a lot wrong in the world around him, including in his own family, and he didn't want to hide from it.

But he reacted with such extreme feelings of overwhelm[1] that he saw no alternative except to withdraw.

It proved helpful to Erich to distinguish between empathy and induced suffering. Empathy doesn't cause us to skip over an article about suffering, to slam shut a book about injustices, or to switch off a TV program about war. Empathy—a loving attitude toward others—motivates us in exactly the opposite direction. It encourages us to know more and to do more.

I urged Erich to think of empathy in entirely positive terms and to view his need to put on blinders as an understandable defense against induced emotional pain. I encouraged him to respect and to value his intelligence, his awareness, and his ethics. The next step, which he began to take, was to decide where he wanted to put his energies. He already wanted to be more available to his wife, and now he felt better able to do that. He also wanted to become more involved in reform projects of his own choosing.

From now on, Erich could approach these aspects of life with the knowledge that empathy is a form of strength and that induced suffering can be understood and overcome. There was a lot of work ahead for him, but now he had the tools to discriminate between the responses he valued and wanted to encourage, and those he didn't.

Erich's conflict is a universal one. Probably every human being at times feels somewhat overwhelmed by the amount of suffering in the world. All human beings have to make decisions about how to respond to suffering and how to allocate their energies. Some people give mostly to their friends and family, others to strangers and to causes. Some people devote much of their lives to helping with the relief of suffering; others try to avoid the issue as much as possible.

Induced emotional suffering, with its associated feelings of helplessness and overwhelm, is a powerful force in human life. It causes us to justify withdrawing from others. It makes us want to close our eyes to the plight of others. It shuts us off from our

---

[1] I first used overwhelm as a noun in *Toxic Psychiatry* to describe the experience of feeling helpless or overcome by painful emotions.

capacities to love and to care. It is a major psychological force in causing human beings to turn away from the suffering of others.

Induced suffering is experienced as a contagion, a form of suffering we catch like a disease from another person. We end up fleeing from the other person as we would flee from a victim of the plague.

One of my colleagues, in agreement with my observations, said he calls the phenomenon "malignant empathy." But he preferred the new term, induced suffering, to make clear its separateness from genuine empathy.

In trying to maintain our healing presence, emotional contagion can be a major obstacle. If we become too upset when our daughter feels upset, we'll worsen her feelings of helplessness. If we become overwhelmed with a fear of death when our friend tells us he's been diagnosed with cancer, we will increase his anxiety.

Induced painful emotions can drive people to injure others. In my work as a medical expert in legal cases, I find that some seemingly callous acts of malpractice are caused in part by induced suffering in the physician or other health providers. Norma's attorney came to me for a consultation in just such a case. Seemingly out of nowhere at the age of 35, Norma had become overwhelmed with anxiety and helplessness. She felt doomed. She drove her husband to distraction by "whining and whimpering." She seemed unable to carry out routine household tasks, even the care of their two young children. With the urging of her mother, she went to a psychiatrist.

Norma had been dominated by her mother and now was being dominated by her husband. Her attempts to rebel enraged her husband and terrified her mother. Norma lapsed into helpless displays of emotional pain in the vain hope of getting help and perhaps to retaliate against those who sought to control her.

Norma's psychiatrist, himself a controlling patriarch, never inquired about the dynamics of Norma's family life. He too wanted to control her—to stop her flagrant suffering—and he prescribed a drug regimen. Eventually he began prescribing large doses of several different medications at once. One night, Norma seemed to drive him to distraction with her piteous wailing on the phone, and he admitted her to the local mental hospital.

In the hospital, Norma paced up and down the ward and stayed up all night. Sleeping pills had little effect. Tranquilizing drugs like Valium flattened her physically and emotionally but provided little relief.

As I read over the hospital record, in retrospect it became apparent that Norma had been upsetting the staff with both her suffering and her difficult behavior. The nurses and aides pressured the doctor for yet more medications. When none of them worked, the doctor decided that Norma wasn't so much anxious as depressed, and he ordered electroshock.

Rendered delirious by the third shock treatment, Norma was still able to inflict emotional pain on those around her. She screamed that the shocks were killing her brain cells—a fact that none of her caregivers wanted to admit. Her psychiatrist in turn increased the intensity of the shocks, until Norma became so mentally disabled that she lay in bed in a fetal position for hours on end.

Norma was discharged from the hospital as "improved." As often happens with shock treatment, she was too brain-injured to continue complaining. It was a relief to everyone: her doctors, her mother, her husband. Everyone approved of the treatment except Norma.

Several years later, Norma was fortunate enough to find a clinical social worker who helped her understand what had been going on all her life in her family dynamics. Norma left her husband, put more distance between herself and her mother, sought new friends, and sued her psychiatrist. No longer depressed, she continued to suffer from brain damage that afflicted her memory and other mental functions. Yet she was emotionally better off. She had learned to be more independent, to take greater responsibility for her life, and to find more nurturing and empowering friends.

There are many perspectives from which to understand Norma's story, from the misguided oppressive treatments of biological psychiatry to the lack of training and patience on the part of the hospital staff. Norma's story can also be understood as an expression of a society that believes in domination and control and that empowers psychiatrists to impose their will on their patients by almost any means.

A more specific aspect of Norma's tragedy is the phenomenon of contagion. Norma's emotional suffering induced intolerable pain in her caregivers, and they in turn ended up going to extremes to shut down or suppress her communications. In doing this, Norma's caregivers were not treating her as much as they were treating themselves. The same was true of Norma's mother and her husband.

If there is one common thread to creating healing presence, it's the importance of understanding and transforming ourselves rather than the other person. This story also illustrates a related theme. Whether we recognize it or not, as helping persons, we too easily and too frequently treat ourselves, while seemingly treating the other person.

Biological psychiatrists, for example, drug, shock, and even lobotomize patients out of the doctors' own needs to control and suppress their patients—often out of their own dreadful fear of intense emotion in themselves. Often the doctors are drugging and shocking away their own guilt, shame, anxiety, and impotence in the face of their patients' suffering. Authoritarian psychotherapists do the same thing, but without damaging their clients' brains. Good or bad, benevolent or malevolent, aware or unaware in our intentions—when we try to treat other people for their emotional problems, we too easily end up treating ourselves at their expense.

In the family, emotional contagion frequently results in child abuse. An infant cries inconsolably and a parent, unable to stand it any longer, assaults or even kills the infant to shut it up. Cases of "euthanasia," in which an elderly spouse murders a sick husband or wife, can be motivated by induced emotional pain.

Distinguishing between induced suffering and empathy is not always easy. When we suffer contagiously over another's pain, it is tempting to call it empathy. It makes our reactions seem noble. But induced suffering instead can make us withdrawn, angry, and even dangerous.

Emotional helplessness is a key in distinguishing feelings of empathy from feelings of induced emotional suffering. The anecdote in chapter 2 about Ginger's rescue of the gull illustrates that a helper can experience painful emotions through empathizing with an injured being without becoming overwhelmed. Ginger actually welcomed the bird's fear and pain as a way of relating to the animal and reassuring it.

Usually we experience induced anguish as an imposition. We resent it and we want to do something to stop it from continuing. If induced suffering goes on for any length of time, it is embittering.

If we are feeling empathic, we accept our own suffering in response to the suffering of others. We feel that we are sharing— helping to lift a burden from the other by allowing ourselves to enter into their experience. Instead of feeling helpless, we feel that we have a purpose.

Empathic suffering, unlike the induced variety, does not over-whelm or paralyze us. It does not feel unwanted or involuntary. It draws out our capacity to pay attention and to love. It does not lead us to take destructive actions to stop others from suffering; instead, it encourages us to engage the person in a life-affirming way. Empathic suffering has a spiritually uplifting purpose. It feels pos-itive rather than futile, and it can bring about confidence and hope in the person who needs our help. When others induce suffering in us, we resent them and want to get away from them. In con-trast, when we feel empathic suffering for another person, we become more loving and want to draw closer to them.

These distinctions between induced and empathic suffering are not black and white. Yet they are meaningful and can help us eval-uate how we are responding in helping situations. They provide another insight into the creation of healing presence.

Induced emotional suffering often has little to do with the other person's real feelings. Because of our own experiences, usually in childhood, we grow sensitive to certain expressions of emotion, and become unable to handle them. Our earlier experiences lead us to misread and to overreact to specific emotions. We may mis-takenly imagine what the other person is feeling and then react to our own false readings.

Many people, for example, grow up with a dread of seeing any uncomfortable emotions on the faces of their family members. In childhood, for example, they learned that painful expressions on their mother's or father's face signalled the beginning of an emo-tional or physical assault. Later in life, if a wife looks angry, her husband may lapse into guilt or humiliation. If a husband looks angry, a wife may be overcome with terror. A smirk on a co-worker's face may drive a man into a frenzy of humiliation and outrage. An expression of hurt feelings may drive someone else into profuse apology. Often the induced emotion is stimulating unconscious memories of childhood trauma, when the same looks on a parent's face warned of impending danger.

Induced suffering usually has more to do with our own past histories than with the real feelings of the other person. When pain is being induced in us, we are usually reacting without understanding what's going on. Genuine empathy instead puts us in touch with the actual inner, subjective experience of the other human being. Usually we find that the other's suffering has little to do with us or that it comes from sources we couldn't anticipate. Often the other person has little awareness of his or her effect on us.

Sometimes, of course, we bear direct responsibility for the suffering of others. Perhaps we have insulted, rejected, or abandoned them. Perhaps we have failed to understand something of great importance to them. But even when we discover that we have contributed to someone else's suffering, we should not allow ourselves to lapse into a helpless, guilt-ridden, or resentful response. It's good to make amends and try to undo the harm. Suffering over our mistakes does not encourage that. Instead, the more we suffer over our mistakes, the less likely we are to admit them or to examine them. If we are too readily induced into suffering, we become perpetual victims. For self-protection, we can end up walling ourselves off from the suffering of others.

When we are feeling genuinely empathic, the other person usually experiences some degree of healing in our presence. Of course we cannot "cure" the person on the spot through empathy, but empathy tends toward healing. Induced suffering usually causes greater upset in the original sufferer. Our pained reaction can make them feel guilty about communicating their suffering to us. It can reconfirm that their suffering is unbearable to anyone. They would be more willing and able to share their pain with someone who isn't overwhelmed by it.

Recent highly publicized studies have shown that men often prove unable to recognize or identify painful emotions on the faces of women. Given the physical science orientation of modern psychiatry and psychology, this gender difference has been attributed to genetics and biology. Instead, the phenomenon is rooted in the social roles of men and women. Helping men change this approach to women is a key to couples therapy.

In my office, from the first few minutes of the first session, it is often apparent that the husband hardly looks at his wife while she's expressing her distress over the marriage. He's either staring into space or looking at me. It takes only a few inquiries from me to elicit from him an explanation. He says that he can't stand to see the pain on his wife's face. It make him feel guilty and ashamed, helpless and frustrated, and angry.

It's not a matter of the man's inability to perceive emotions. The emotions, including tears and muffled sobs, would draw attention from across a crowded room. It takes effort *not* to recognize them.

Why are so many men so seemingly unwilling or unable to respond to the feelings of women? Before attempting an answer, it's instructive to note that women often do the opposite with men. They frequently study the faces of their husbands and boyfriends to ferret out every nuance of emotion. Some do it as if their lives depend on it. In therapy, for example, it's not uncommon to watch a woman study her husband's face to anticipate and to fend off any show of anger or even disappointment with her.

What's going on? Much can be understood in terms of the domination and control that adult males, throughout most of history, have exerted over women and children. This domination occurs in both family and society. Men, because of their advantages in authority and power, have been able to handle conflict by ignoring or suppressing the feelings of other family members.

When men see pain in the faces of their wives and children, they are likely to experience it as induced suffering. That is, they too often cannot respond empathically. Instead, they react as if the other person's emotions are inflicting needless pain on them. Too often, men have simply not learned how to respond to suffering in a caring or nurturing fashion. They react to suffering in the family as an imposition or even as a weapon against them in conflict situations.

Women and children, lacking in power and authority and experiencing much more vulnerability, have been compelled to pay excruciating attention to the feelings of men. There have been dire consequences for any failure to respond to the adult male's changing moods.

Because women and children often feel helpless in relation to men, they will experience their husband's and father's emotions as induced suffering. Overcome by fear and other negative emotions, women and children will not be able to respond empathically.

Even among couples who do not personally accept traditional male and female roles, husbands and wives are likely to react in these typical ways. These attitudes have been indoctrinated into them while growing up and reinforced in school and the workplace. As one of my university students recently pointed out, when a male student so much as grunts, the class's attention goes toward him, while a female student can wave her hand to no avail.

Neither men nor women, under these conditions, can be very empathic toward the other. Empathy between men and women—or between any two people—requires a degree of equality, including similar degrees of power, authority, and vulnerability. Otherwise, emotions become a method for inducing pain in each other in the hope of gaining the upper hand. At this point in family life, communications become a form of mutual torture.

Children, despite our occasional idealization of them, are rarely as capable of empathy as adults. They are too vulnerable to the adults around them. Empathy, especially empathic self-transformation, requires an underlying sense of identity, of self-control, of mastery. One cannot feel empathic while also feeling small and powerless. Children are bound to feel fearful, helpless, or needy much of the time and, therefore, are largely focused on themselves rather than on others.

This is not to say that children cannot feel empathy. By one or two years of age, many children show a response that seems very similar to adult empathy. If another child cries, the empathic youngster may toddle over to offer a pat or a hug or even a favorite stuffed animal. One can see from the empathic child's face that he or she isn't suffering. The child may be smiling as he or she hurries over to offer help. It is a loving response rather than induced suffering. The full flowering of empathic self-transformation, however, requires adulthood. It draws on wisdom and understanding, and the strength and willingness to respond to the psychological, social, and spiritual needs of others. We must have insight into our own needs and how to care for them before we can fully respond to the needs of others. Otherwise, we are likely to withdraw from other people's suffering in order to control our own overwhelming reactions to it.

Angela, "the sad little angel" whom we met earlier in this chapter, felt empowered by the concept of empathic self-transformation. This discussion of induced suffering then put her in touch with who she had been as a child—the little girl who seemingly felt too much. In adulthood, when one of her friends or family was suffering, she sensed it poignantly within herself and sometimes withdrew from it. Faced with a series of painful illnesses and deaths among her friends, the suffering of others finally exhausted her.

Now Angela began to understand how the overwhelming intensity of her emotional reactions was rooted in her own unfulfilled spiritual needs. All of her life, Angela had felt utterly alone. No one ever seemed to be there to confirm her special love and awareness of life. Later in life, when someone reached out to her, she withdrew to protect herself from repeated disappointment and further abandonment.

Now, in therapy, it became clear to her that she needed to nurture her own spirit before she could bear to reach out to others who were suffering. Drawing on the concept of empathic self-transformation, she said to me, "I need to be the center of my own attention." She laughed and said, "Put that phrase in your book—I need to be the center of my own attention. I need to take care of myself before I can give myself fully to other people."

Angela's focus on herself was important at that moment in her life but, as she also knew, there is a reciprocity between concern for self and concern for others. We harm ourselves when we focus too exclusively on our own needs. We end up feeling defensive and isolated. We receive little in return from others. We lose our capacity to bond with others.

Because of our social nature, we nurture ourselves when we nurture others and we empower ourselves when we empower others. When we find new psychological and spiritual resources within ourselves in order to help others, at the same time we encourage our own growth and development.

Empathic self-transformation is not sacrificial. It opens us to new aspects of ourselves as we further our capacity to relate to the emotional and spiritual needs of others.

Does Empathy Make Us Too Vulnerable?   6

If we are empathic, won't other people take advantage of us? How can empathy help us defend ourselves from others? How can love for one person strengthen our capacity to love others?

Big Joe is an enormous, even ominous man—tall, broad-shouldered, and thick of girth. He once worked as a bouncer. Years ago he was in the marines. What's his greatest fear in regard to shedding his menacing exterior?

"They'll think I'm a pushover. People will walk all over me."

Not a chance. Nobody, ever, will think that Big Joe is an easy mark. He could work overtime learning to be more aware of others, and the impression at best would be that of a gentle but potentially ominous grizzly bear.

Where did Joe get his fears? Like all of us, he too once was small. Like most of us, he was taken advantage of in sundry ways, including physical and sexual abuse at the hands of larger children. Joe made up his mind. As soon as he got big enough, "Nobody's going to mess with me."

Big Joe can tell me his height and weight; but he cannot imagine the impression of hugeness he makes on others. He reacts to people as if he's a slight 10-year-old boy peeking out from within a mountainous body. I stood beside him one day toward the end of our session and said, "Look at the size of you. I've got good shoulders but yours are half-again as wide. And you're a foot taller."

Joe shook his head. He heard my words; he was looking down on the top of my thinning head of hair. But he couldn't grasp his monumental size or imposing carriage.

Joe learned to soften his masquerade of invulnerability. He found that it turned out all right—that he actually was treated with as much or more respect than ever, and with much more affection. Eventually it became clear that by acting in a menacing fashion, he had threatened other men, some of whom tried to threaten him back. Nowadays his sheer size tends to make people grateful for his gentleness of demeanor.

Most of us fear what would happen if we gave up our habitual ways of armoring and defending ourselves. Some of us use a sharp tongue or glib remark and others a stony silence. Some rely on a subtle smirk or an arrogant sneer and others on a shy, downcast look to feign harmlessness. Some become aggressive and others withdraw. Some use steel-trap logic to fend off others and others rely on emotional outbursts. Some of us polish up our posture and dress to an extreme to make others treat us respectfully; some slouch and dress down to avoid attention or competition.

Although the source of our vulnerabilities is usually hidden in childhood amnesia, we fear repetitions of early experiences when we felt manipulated and controlled by others. If we allow ourselves to become empathic, to connect, or to bond, we fear we will be taken advantage of. At the mercy of other people, we'll be made to feel guilty, anxious, or ashamed.

What really happens is far more dismal. In our compulsive efforts to protect ourselves, we lose track of our capacity to feel our own feelings or to pay attention to the feelings of others. Our protective posturing often draws negative attention, embroiling us in unwanted conflict. Our defenses become self-defeating, wrongly confirming for us that we need them after all.

It's important to learn that being empathic or caring doesn't mean being manipulated. A genuine empathy instead tends to put us in touch with what other people are really feeling. Our own authenticity sets their lack of it into more clear relief. If they have hostile intentions or hidden agendas in regard to us, we are much more likely to sense them if we are fully open to our feelings as well as to theirs.

By becoming less responsive to others, we wall ourselves off from their emotional signals—including their negative ones. By remaining open to feelings, we remain alert for danger signals, including hostile and loveless attitudes.

When there is a clear and present danger from others, we may have to take defensive measures. Usually we can do this without inflicting any harm on the other person. Under emotional assault, we can gently try to disarm the other person, we can point out that they're making us uncomfortable, and when necessary, we can remove ourselves from them. Often we can create the potential for a more respectful and loving interchange.

I was taking a cab from the airport to my home one evening when the cabby seemed to be driving somewhat recklessly, crawling up the backs of other cars and weaving in and out too speedily. As he stopped for a traffic light, I said to him as mildly as I could, "It feels to me as if you're going a little too fast—not very fast, but a little too much for me to relax."

The driver turned around and said in a heavy Indian accent, "Angry! Angry!" He seemed to be shaking his fist.

I was taken back, and said, "I'm sorry if I made you angry. I've had a very long day, flying back and forth, and I need to relax on my way home."

"Not angry," he said, "angry, angry!" At least, that's what it sounded like, until I realized he was gesticulating at his mouth.

"Hungry?" I asked. "You're hungry?"

"Yes," he smiled. " I'm 'ungry. I have not eaten all day."

We were driving once again, a little more slowly, and I said, "I must be your last fare of the day, and you won't eat 'til you get home."

"Yes," he said. "Very hungry."

"I have a bag of pretzels from the airplane. May I give them to you?" I offered. "They're low fat—not a bad snack."

"Oh, for me?" he was genuinely surprised.

He ended up snacking on the pretzels and chatting amiably (I could hardly understand a word) all the way home.

When we got to my house, I paid him the amount of the fare, and then asked if he would give me change for a $20 bill so I could give him a tip. He waved off the tip, thanked me, and wished me a pleasant evening.

A disarming intervention will not always lead to a complete reversal, ending in conviviality; but it will usually terminate an attack. On the phone, I was being treated very shabbily by someone I'd never met. Instead of hanging up, I asked in all sincerity, "Is there some reason you've disliked me from the start of this call?"

The man was so startled that he ended up mumbling that he'd done nothing wrong. Before I could say anything else, he quickly gave me the information I needed and hung up.

A gentle empathic attitude is often enough to soothe people with good intentions and to drive away people.with more hostile intentions. They see their anger and emotional violence mirrored in our greater calm and become uncomfortable with themselves. In a sense, by "being peace" we confront them with how they are being something else.

If we radiate a healing, peaceful, or loving presence, this in itself will usually reduce the amount of hostility and conflict that is generated around us. I have worked in and consulted with hospital programs, treating similar populations of patients that have very different problems with violence. Where the patients are treated with dignity and respect, there is relatively little or no need to resort to forced injections of drugs, straitjackets, or isolation rooms. Where patients are treated as inferiors in need of control, the staff ends up concluding that a hospital cannot function without a variety of oppressive measures.

There are, of course, exceptions to this optimistic principle. Sometimes disturbed and even dangerous people will be attracted to empathic human beings and, at the least, make unreasonable demands on them. There are times when, with our emotional backs to the wall, we need to define ourselves in sharp distinction to others. We may find ourselves saying, "Back off. Give me space. Stop what you are doing to me."

Nipping or flicking a hoof at creatures who impinge on us is a characteristic of all social animals. Any animal that hangs around with other creatures of its own kind retains some capacity to push them out of its space. Antlers lowered in a menacing way, a hoof snapped out dangerously, a tooth bared, a tail twitched, a neck arched—these signals are usually sufficient to reestablish a comfortable distance.

My wife, Ginger, and I laid out a long line of sunflower seeds on our back sidewalk. Six squirrels lined up along the trail of seeds, each occupying exactly 3 feet of space. Outside the line, other squirrels waited to replace or to displace one of the feeding animals. The newly arrived squirrel would take up exactly the same 3 feet. If another squirrel encroached, there was a brief dispute, until one was chased off.

This same routine is repeated by the various species of birds that come to the feeders. Typically, they are more aggressive toward their own kind than toward birds of another feather.

"Leave me alone!" or "My space!" or "Don't mess with me!" are important self-defining moments in social beings. Children struggle over when and how to say it, and how to make others pay attention to it. Parents suffer from confusion and doubt about when to allow their children this defining moment and when instead to say, "The play room is for everyone," or "You can't hog the whole couch," or "You need to sit on your side of the car seat."

For human beings, a safe space extends beyond physical dimensions. It requires a safe emotional environment. To defend that space, we often have to do the equivalent of snarling or baring our teeth in response to incursions of all kinds, including subtle emotional assaults.

To be sensitive, to be aware, to be empathic—is not to be defenseless. Instead, with our antenna better tuned to the world of people around us, we're more able to select those with whom it's safe to risk intimacy. We become more able to identify and to ward off dangerous individuals or damaging interchanges, while we also learn to spot and to welcome more loving people and communications.

In therapy, teaching, and friendship, I explain that accusatory, hostile, or threatening behavior makes it difficult for me to remain open and empathic. I try to help my client, student, or friend find another way to communicate, including any complaints about me, without trying to injure me emotionally.

Ginger and I often work on the same floor of the same house much of the day. Our assistant is likely to be there, too. Often there are teenagers around and sometimes visitors. It's commonplace for one of us to get testy or grumpy, indicating that the space at that moment has gotten too tight. "Back off!" we're saying to the others.

I pointed out that hostile people are likely to avoid us when we're being more peaceful with ourselves and others. This applies to us as well. If we are hostile or defensive, we will tend to avoid more positive people. We become too aware of our perpetrations against others when we are in close proximity to people who are more in touch with their loving nature.

The more open to people we become, the more opportunity we have in making friends. Obviously, we also will be more effective in connecting to the positive qualities of anyone we are trying to help as a therapist, teacher, parent, or friend.

I like to describe therapy as a mini-utopia, a space in which the therapist and client can relate to each other in safety. Sometimes clients want to "dump" on their therapists. The maxim seems to be, "If I can't scream at my own therapist, who can I scream at?" I don't think "unloading" on people is ever helpful, even in therapy. Therapy should be a safe haven. In keeping with what I've been saying throughout this book, it should be safe for the therapist as well as the client in order for the therapist to be fully available.

It's possible to make therapy an especially safe, and, hence helpful setting. Earlier in the book, we looked at one of the keys— placing ethical restraints on ourselves as therapists, especially in what we can expect from our clients or patients. It may seem artificial to have a "paid friendship" with a professional person. Instead, the constraints and limits built into therapy make it more effective than friendship in dealing with emotional turmoil and overwhelm.

Although it's much more complicated to do so in our private lives, we can strive to make our personal relationships as ideal as possible—to base our friendships and our family lives on mutual respect, empathy, and love. Utopian? Yes. But what is life about if not about the effort to live by ethical and loving principles?

Can empathy cause us to become obsessively attached to one person at the expense of family, society, or humanity? A recent scientific column quoted an "expert" who believes that to the degree we feel empathy toward our own group, we are likely to feel exaggerated hostility toward another. Is this so—that empathy for one group generates defensive hate for another?

Similarly, it is sometimes said that falling in love cuts us off from other people. And surely it is true that in the blush of romance, lovers can temporarily lose interest in everyone else. Does that mean that love for one person in the long run motivates isolation from others?

Sometimes parents think that devotion to their children makes them ferociously protective of them, even at the expense of other children or adults. Can empathy therefore turn us into proverbial tigers in defense of our own? In other words, can empathy for one person lead us to make less of another?

It can help to pose the question in different ways. If a mother loves her infant with all her heart, is it likely to make her more sensitive or less sensitive to the feelings of other children? If a man is devoted to his wife, will that make him more or less caring toward other women?

Empathy begins on a very personal level but by its very nature encourages us to expand our circle of concern. An infant experiences parental love, feels secure in that love, and then, learns to love. Eventually that love expands to include others outside of mom and dad. I have seen this happen time and again in adulthood as well. The love we feel for those who are closest to us expands to include others. It's a basic principle of psychotherapy that a person can experience feelings of love within the therapy that open the possibility for experiencing yet more love outside the office. Love for one person thus encourages us to become more loving toward all people.

Why is this so? When we love others, we love them as they are. It is unconditional. We love them not only warts and all, but nasty, self-centered intentions and all. We love them despite, and even because of, the inherent flaws and contradictions that plague all human beings. We love them when they are feeling generous and when they are feeling selfish. We love them when they are brave and when they are cowardly; when they are brilliant and when they are stupid; when they are physically beautiful and when they are ravaged by illness and age. And we love them not only because they are so much like us but because they are so different.

Having loved one person in this way, it becomes difficult to reject others on the grounds that they are different, selfish, cowardly, stupid, or ugly. After all, that's how, at times, we perceive our loved one to be.

But if our love is idealized, if we imagine divine perfection where in fact only a touch of divinity can be found, then we are not truly empathic toward our loved one. If we want to imagine that our loved one is free of physical and moral blemishes, then we are likely to resent others who remind us of the universality of these defects.

If we make believe that our child is unique among children in deserving to be cherished, if we make believe that our loved one is unique among adults in deserving to be treasured, if we make believe that our group is unique among groups in deserving to prosper and survive—this is not love but self-deception. We exaggerate the perfection of our loved one in order to inflate our own flagging self-esteem.

Freud thought romantic love was a delusional overestimation of the value of the other. He called passionate love an extension of narcissism, an overinflation of our own value. The great American psychologist and philosopher, William James, similarly concluded that romantic love was a monomania. Freud and James were expressing common misconceptions about love.

Genuine love does not idealize our loved one above all others, it includes our loved one in humanity. We do not fail to perceive the flaws in our loved ones; we accept and even enjoy them as aspects or expressions of their lives.

Genuine love, including the empathy that goes along with it, reaches to the common humanity of our loved one. It loves the other for his or her unique qualities, but also for those ordinary ones. It reaches to what's special in our loved one, but recognizes that being unique is itself a shared human characteristic.

Many people love their pets very dearly. I know a number of devoted dog owners who get together on a regular basis with other dog owners. Almost invariably these people recognize that Jane loves her terrier with the same devotion that they love their spaniel. Almost invariably they recognize that the terrier deserves as much love as the spaniel. Sure, Shetland sheepdogs have a special place in my heart; but it's hard to imagine that they are the only breed deserving of such affection.

As I've said earlier, it's sometimes easier to see the humanity in animals than in people. That's because we're less threatened by animals. It may also be that they are more willing and able to express love in a direct, unadulterated manner. Because we're less threatened, and because they are more open and vulnerable, we become more open to love and to empathy. Similarly, many people find it much easier to love an infant or a small child than to love an adult.

As a small child, I very much loved my dog, Pitch. Once when he was injured and hampered by a cast, he was attacked by another rather dangerous dog, a large boxer. I intervened and drove the other dog away. At the moment, I felt no fear for myself, but only for my dog. Yet I didn't feel hatred for the dread boxer. I didn't want to hurt him; I only wanted to drive him off. After all, he was a dog, too, and I loved dogs.

When we are driven to hatred and violence because of threats against our loved ones, it's not because of how much we love; instead, in our threatened state, we have forsaken love, and become hateful. Yes, love does bring out the protectiveness in us—the desire to secure our loved ones from harm. But it doesn't motivate us to unleash wanton harm on others. Any time love is used to justify violence or hate, be skeptical. A loving person abhors violence toward anyone or anything.

Love is the spiritual glue of humanity. It may be the primary energy of life. Although I've made some efforts in that direction in *Beyond Conflict*, I don't have a complete philosophy of love. Instead, I have experiences, honed by research and reasoning. Experience has taught me that love is a vital principle of life. To love is to participate as fully as we can in life—to take joy in life, to be caring toward life, to nurture and protect life. Healing people through caring relationships is among the most life-affirming opportunities.

Beyond the Quick and Easy Cure

7

What's wrong with seeking a quick and easy way of fixing our emotional and spiritual problems? Why shouldn't we do everything possible to relieve emotional pain in ourselves and other people?

Rita arrived for her first appointment with me, an initial consultation about the psychiatric drugs she had been taking for years. She was on Prozac for her depressed feelings, Klonopin for her anxious ones, and Dalmane to sleep at night. Sometimes she also took Dexedrine to help her wake up and get going.

As we started to discuss her life, Rita attributed her anxious feelings to insufficient Klonopin, her blue feelings to not enough of Prozac, her difficulties sleeping to a need for more Dalmane, and her sluggishness in the morning to insufficient Dexedrine. Rita could not complete a thought about how she was feeling without mentioning a drug and wondering about her supposed biochemical imbalances.

"How are the afternoons going for you?" I asked about her sometimes difficult days at home with her daughter.

"I think my morning Klonopin begins to wear off by 3 PM," she responded.

"What are the evenings like for you with your husband?" I continued.

"It depends on how quickly the Dalmane kicks in," she replied.

In the first several sessions, I could not get her to talk about her feelings as something separable from her drugs.

The drugs had begun with her internist giving her Dalmane to help her sleep. While the Dalmane, a minor tranquilizer, helped her sleep for the first week, she began to notice her anxiety level going up during the day. Her internist then referred her to a psychiatrist. Instead of suspecting that the increased daytime anxiety might be a drug-withdrawal reaction to the Dalmane wearing off, her psychiatrist started her on Klonopin. He told her she had a biochemical imbalance causing her insomnia and her anxiety. As she got depressed he added Prozac with an occasional Dexedrine to help her get going in the morning.

Working with her previous psychiatrist, Rita's life became a matter of pharmacological brain tinkering. Each day, each hour of her life was focused on balancing her drugs to balance her brain chemistry.

Rita could not have guessed that her psychiatrist's theories were wholly made up—that nothing was abnormal in her brain before the drugs were poured into her system. Ironically, now she had innumerable biochemical imbalances, each of them induced by drugs.

My efforts with Rita started from psychospiritual scratch. I explained to her that as long as her brain was soaked in medications she would find it impossible to figure out which of her emotional responses were caused by her problems and which were caused by toxic drug reactions in her brain.

Regardless of the origin of Rita's emotional pain at any given time, her understanding of her emotions had become lost in the toxic fog. Half the time her brain was responding to the rising levels of drugs in her bloodstream; the other half of the time, it was responding to the diminishing blood levels between doses. Since the drugs had different rates of removal from her body, she was exposed to an unpredictable tide of rising and falling medication levels in her blood and brain. In addition, the drugs were interacting with each other, affecting how the body handled them. As I describe in several other books, including *Toxic Psychiatry* (1991), *Talking Back to Prozac* (1994, with Ginger Breggin) and *Brain-Disabling Treatments in Psychiatry* (1997), Rita's brain was also producing compensatory reactions to each of the drugs, resulting in complex, unpredictable interactions that far exceed current scientific under-standing.

In retrospect, Rita realized that her drug-oriented psychiatrist had never discussed even the most obvious causes of her sleep problems, such as worries about her marriage staying together and concerns about problems with her children. He never asked about her ambitions or goals for herself.

In the process of gradually removing the drugs, one by one, we found they were doing more harm than good. Only when free of all of the drugs was Rita able to examine and to guide her own life, her thoughts and feelings, including the conflicts with her husband and her children that were originally keeping her awake at night. It turned out that she wanted her husband more involved in the child-rearing, while she made plans to go back to school.

"Got an emotional problem? Whatever it is, there's a drug for you." As Rita's case illustrates, that's the quick-fix approach of mod-ern psychiatry. Prozac for depression, Xanax for anxiety, lithium for the emotional ups and downs, a cocktail of everything if one or two don't do the trick. Psychiatric drugs have become our fast food for the soul.

Even so-called talking doctors have gotten into the act. Gone are the days when a psychotherapist was seen as a source of wisdom, insight, and understanding. Now he or she is expected to provide formulae for better living, along with a referral to a physician for medication.

Insurance companies, HMOs, and Preferred Provider Organiza-tions have become enforcers of the quick fix. If it can't be done on a mental health assembly line, they don't want to fund it.

The quick-fix attitude doesn't stop with mental health profes-sionals. It percolates throughout society. Nowadays people have begun to view each other the way biological psychiatrists view their patients.

"I feel depressed," our friend tells us.

"You probably have a biochemical imbalance," we respond, ending our responsibility as a friend.

"I feel anxious," says another friend.

We recommend a doctor who prescribes Xanax, ending the need for further conversation.

Will there ever be a quick cure for life's pain and anguish? Probably not. Our oldest literature, predating the Bible and the Homeric poems, suggests that we have always struggled. So do the myths of indigenous peoples. Now we endure an irony worth underscoring: In the face of increasing complexity in modern life, we seek ever more simple-minded solutions.

Our lives could be lived as heroic stories, filled with mystery and ripe with potential tragedy and triumph. Instead they are lived as periodic bouts with mental illness.

Psychiatry is largely to blame for translating the human struggle into "biochemical imbalances" suitable for treatment with medication or even shock treatment. Nearly every psychiatrist has become a technological doctor feelgood. There is, however, fertile soil for this drug-oriented approach in a society that is morally and spiritually at sea.

Why are people driven to accept such simple-minded medical approaches to their suffering? Many reasons have combined to reinforce our faith in the new technology of brain and mind. Our ancient mythologies have withered. We have replaced them with false gods, in particular biological science and laboratory technology, as the answer to human psychological, social, and spiritual problems. This is an extension of the overall materialism which dominates our society. We use drugs like Prozac to help us shut down our feelings while we pursue making money at a feverish pitch.

Adults have lost faith in traditional sources of knowledge. These sources of knowledge have lost faith in themselves. Nowadays when most priests, ministers, or rabbis confront a truly despairing member of their flock—for example, someone on the verge of suicide—they refer the person to a psychiatrist for "real" help.

Yet there was a time when psychological and spiritual help was real help. Religious faith was rooted in the conviction that religion could provide, if not answers, then solace in the face of life's most fearful mental and spiritual threats. Nowadays if Moses experienced God in a burning bush or a column of fire, he wouldn't bring God's word to the Jews; he'd take himself to a psychiatrist. If Paul heard voices on the road to Tarsus, he wouldn't convert to Christianity; he'd have himself committed to a mental hospital. In more modern times, if George Fox fell into years of despair and depression, he wouldn't found the Quakers, he'd take Prozac, Zoloft, or Paxil, probably in combination with Xanax or Klonopin. What once was God's turf is now monopolized by psychiatrists and drugs.

The same, unfortunately, is true for psychology and philosophy. William James, the great 19th century American thinker, embodied the combined roles of physician, psychologist, philosopher, and religious thinker. His most inspired book, *The Varieties of Religious Experience*, found that each of us is essentially incomplete and yearns for merger with God. His descriptions of this merger, if subjected to psychiatric diagnosis, would fit well into the various categories of mental illness. That didn't bother him; he didn't feel obliged to hand over spiritual crises to psychiatrists.

Nowadays William James would probably end up referring his most disturbed clients to his psychiatric colleagues down the hall. God would remain a distant abstraction to him, seemingly irrelevant to issues of profound despair.

My intention is not to promote or to criticize organized religion, although I do wish it would not relegate the "curing of souls" to psychiatry. I am Jewish and believe that life at root is an ethical and spiritual adventure. I believe there's something greater going on than my mere brain chemistry, or even my own autonomous will, but I don't pretend to know exactly who or what it is. I am sure that there is a deeper meaning to life and that the meaning has something to do with responsibility and with love, as well as with acknowledging the value of every human life.

Some of my clients may have relatively little conscious awareness of my ethical or spiritual values. They may have shown little direct interest in these matters and I would not attempt to push my views on them. In therapy, I try to work on the frontiers of my clients' personal experiences, encouraging them to push forward in their own chosen directions.

Although I may not communicate at any length with all of my clients about my ethical or spiritual values, I hope that I am presenting them through my demeanor in the sessions. If I am successful in developing a healing presence, I will be demonstrating through my way of being with my clients that I cherish and value them, and wish to promote their well-being and happiness. I will be showing them that I believe in courteous, thoughtful, respect-ful, empathic relationships.

Whether we intend it or not, we do communicate our values by how we relate to people. The therapist who tries to be "objective" is communicating a very definite set of values that may in fact injure the clients by reaffirming that no one can care about them, even their own therapist.

Regardless of how people feel about specific values or ideals, a satisfying, successful life, by almost any standard, requires a con-scious awareness and application of sound principles. This is true for those of us who live without much abstract speculation and for those of us who are intellectually or religiously preoccupied. Whether our criteria for success require feeling good about our-selves or contributing to others, or both, successful human beings measure, monitor, and guide everyday life by ethical principles.

Life isn't easy for anyone. Recently I was debating a psychiatrist at a public forum in Toronto. To justify increased public support for psychiatry, he cited a Canadian survey which found that 20% of the citizens of the province at one time or another in their lives were "disabled" by a mental illness. I responded that the real fig-ure was 100%—that being "mentally disabled" some of the time went with the human turf. There was confirmatory laughter and applause from the audience.

From my knowledge of my friends and clients and from litera-ture of every kind, it is apparent that almost all people at some time in their lives feel at the edge of the spiritual void. Almost every sentient human being has wanted, at times, to give up the struggle or has wished for death. At such times, people can experi-ence epiphanies of insight and make life-transforming decisions. By contrast, those people who do manage to go through life seem-ingly without profound conflict are probably living like horses with blinders. They fulfill their duties and obligations along a rela-tively narrow and uninspired path while someone else holds the reins. Nowadays it's usually a psychiatrist at the biochemical reins.

Nationally syndicated TV and radio talk-show host Rush Lim-baugh and I have very different political outlooks, but we share some important values, including our mutual emphasis on per-sonal responsibility and the importance of living by values. That we do share these ideals indicates the importance of principled living across the spectrum of American viewpoints (chapter 13).

Although Rush rarely does anything like this, he invited me to be interviewed as an expert on one of his radio shows. The initial subject was the drugging of America's children with psychiatric medications like Ritalin. He and I agreed that turning to biopsychiatric treatment was an abrogation of family values and personal responsibility for our children. Then, to my surprise, he also wanted to talk about adults who take Prozac. With great sincerity, Limbaugh spoke about how he had become very depressed earlier in his life and how Prozac had been urged on him. Instead of Prozac, he explained to his 22 million listeners, he rejected the idea of drugs and chose to remake his life. He was grateful that he did.

Psychiatrists often argue that being "mentally ill" is different from struggling with life on a psychological and spiritual level. Conflicts over the meaning of life, according to these experts, don't make people so "clinically" depressed that they require psychiatric help to go on living.

In reality, people live and die by their principles, however confused, contradictory, or unconscious these principles may be. The woman who is so depressed that she can't get out of bed is feeling overwhelmed by the prospect of facing her life. What could bring her to such a desperate state? Her conflicted feelings about her life.

Subtle, complex motives often determine why people remain so depressed that they would rather stay in bed, die, or go to a state mental hospital than face their lives. Often, it's due in part to the unconscious resurfacing of intolerable memories of childhood abuse, perhaps restimulated in adulthood by the continued presence and influence of the offending parent, by the birth or development of children, or by events in a marriage. Often it has to do with unbearably violent impulses felt toward members of their own family, including children or a spouse. Sometimes an illicit passion for a forbidden person, known only to the sufferer, can motivate self-hate and futility, leading to severe depression. Commonly, depression is caused by subtle yet devastating emotional abuse from another family member.

Deep despair is frequently caused by forbidden desires, such as the desire for love or for more courageous choices in life. A father and husband wishes to give up his compulsive devotion to work. He wants instead to pursue more fulfilling activities at a pace that allows him to enjoy life; but he lapses into profound guilt at the prospect of depriving his wife and children of their accustomed high standard of living. A mother wants to stand up to her husband about the brutal treatment he inflicts on their children; but she becomes paralyzed by self-doubt, guilt, and fear.

Life-and-death conflicts are usually fought and lost on such an internal level that no one knows of their existence—sometimes not even the person who is enduring them. Typically, the person's own mind has become so murky with depression, or so confused by conflicting emotions, that he or she has no idea why life has come to a dead end. The emotional paralysis is meant to obscure or to ward off the overwhelming emotional conflict. Drugs or shock treatment only worsens the individual's detachment from himself or herself.

Subtle or gross forms of abuse; frustrated values, dreams, and ideals; painful childhood experiences that become reactivated by adult experiences—these are the stuff of life-and-death conflicts. Compared to these conflicts, biochemical imbalances are but figments of the psychiatric imagination.

The same principles apply to all psychiatric disorders, from "panic disorder" to "schizophrenia." At the root of each lies a personal story about heroism or failed heroism in dealing with the challenge of life, about spiritual capacity and incapacity, about ethical confusion and contradiction, and ultimately about the struggle to create a life of satisfaction and meaning.

The same principles also apply to lesser intensities of emotional overwhelm. More subtle degrees of anxiety or depression, for example, are likely rooted in hidden trauma and misunderstood or conflicted principles of living.

Those who are suffering often shrink from help that might clarify the deeper sources of their problems. After all, those emotional wellsprings have left them feeling overwhelmed. These clients, desperately afraid of dealing with emotions, need encouragement not to turn to quick fixes that will further alienate them from their inner life. They are easy marks for any doctor who offers them a drug.

Even if the person wants psychospiritual help, there may be no one available to spend the time or energy. Friends usually do not have the training, experience, patience, or time to offer help to people in states of despair. Besides, healing often requires a more protected and specialized relationship, such as psychotherapy. Unfortunately, too many mental health professionals—including biological psychiatrists—also lack the capacity to help. These psychiatrists hide their lack of healing presence behind medical diagnoses, mental hospitalization, and physical interventions.

What is society to do? *We* are society. Keep in mind that we must first help ourselves before we can fully help others. We must be in a spiritual condition that promotes our own well-being. Then we can move on to create genuinely helpful conditions for other human beings. To the extent that we can apply the principle of empathic self-awareness to ourselves, we can become more helpful to others through our very presence.

Meanwhile, it's unfortunate that psychotherapy is becoming more difficult to obtain. Insurance programs are providing less and less coverage for it. Therapists themselves often seem to feel compelled to recommend physicians who can prescribe drugs. The expense of psychotherapy without insurance is too high for most people.

One solution requires recognizing the real qualities required for becoming a good psychotherapist. Advanced degrees, such as an M.D. or Ph.D., contribute little or nothing to a person's ability to do therapy. Instead, contemporary academic training and supervision can stifle intuitive skills and spontaneous caring. The competitiveness of the academic process winnows out more empathic people in favor of more obsessive and competitive ones. The arduous and largely irrelevant training required to obtain professional credentials encourages the graduates to demand higher prices for their services. The difficulty of getting the required degrees and the myth that the degrees confer an automatic level of expertise allow professionals to create licensure monopolies to enforce their higher prices.

Mature adults—with or without academic credentials—could be easily trained in psychotherapy institutes in two or three years time. An especially good source of candidates would be among women who had completed raising their children or men and women who had reached retirement age. If a college degree and superior academic performance were not requirements for admission to these institutes, candidates could be selected on the basis of more relevant human capacities, such as personal responsibility, empathy, and healing presence. The potentially large number of graduates from these psychotherapy training institutes would create a much more competitive marketplace with more and better therapists. The price of psychotherapy would go down, while the quality would go up. Economic pressure for a quick and easy cure would be reduced. Therapists would be more readily available to provide the help that people really need and crave.

Life is complex, often confusing, and inherently ethical and spiritual in nature. The most satisfying life requires that we guide ourselves and others with sound principles, such as the fulfillment of basic needs, honesty, and empathy. There is no ethical shortcut to happiness or a fulfilling life.

From Fear and Helplessness to Love

8

What does it mean, "We are all born into fear and helplessness?" Why is this so important to know in helping ourselves and other people?

Recently the movie star who played Superman, Christopher Reeve, was paralyzed in a horseback riding accident. It sent shudders through many of us. Not only did we feel empathy for him, many felt threatened by the image of the super hero reduced to helplessness. We wondered how he could bear to go on living.

A paralyzed adult can be as physically helpless as an infant. Safety and survival hang by the thread of how much attention he or she can get from other people. Yet, as Reeve began to show us, being physically helpless is not the same as being psychologically or spiritually helpless.

As Reeve began his partial physical recovery, he made public appearances. We were once again inspired by him, this time with his real life courage as he used his disability as a vehicle for communicating hope. We witnessed a man's triumph over the most extreme physical adversity. He became, surely more than ever, a hero.

The story of Reeve exemplifies an important psychological reality: there is an enormous difference between physical helplessness and emotional or spiritual helplessness. Similarly, there is a vast difference between the constraints imposed on us by reality, including death and taxes, and those imposed on us by ourselves and our emotional reactions.

Infants begin life in a state of almost total physical helplessness. An infant cannot feed itself, cannot dry or clean itself, cannot ward off the bite of an insect or the stick of a pin. Most important, it cannot touch, cuddle, and love itself. When it tries to satisfy itself—for example, through compulsive rocking or self-stimulation—it is reaching a state of desperation.

Yet from the beginning, a healthy infant is not emotionally helpless. An infant can attract attention to its needs by crying loudly. As it matures, an infant and child can learn more winning ways than crying. It will coo and smile, eliciting needed nurturing responses from adults. But in the beginning, its most effective communication is to cry. When it gets down to rock-bottom expressions of need, the same is probably true for adults.

When healthy infants are abandoned to institutional care where their basic emotional needs are not met, they eventually lapse into emotional helplessness. In the absence of consistent nurturing, including caring physical contact and love, they give up trying to get it. After going through stages that resemble anger and anxiety, they display something closely resembling depression as we know it in adults. As I review in *Beyond Conflict,* some of these infants stop eating and responding to adult overtures, and die. Similar life-threatening reactions are seen among some adults in extreme situations of deprivation and systematic abuse, such as prisoner-of-war and concentration camps.

These responses reflect emotional or psychological helplessness. Other forms of helplessness, such as physical paralysis or an infant's physical limitations, are objective. They are caused by realities outside ourselves rather than by our attitudes. We are all objectively helpless in the face of inevitable death.

The *feeling* of helplessness is different from objective helplessness. Behind emotional or psychological helplessness lies a subjective judgment about our own personal capacity to handle ourselves and our lives. As the life of South African leader Nelson Mandela dramatizes, even an imprisoned man can maintain enormous control over his own spiritual condition—so much so that he eventually influences the condition of a whole nation and even the world.

As a healing person, nothing is more crucial than encouraging people to overcome their feelings of helplessness. Helplessness reflects a judgment about ourselves that nothing can be done, that all is lost, that there's no sense trying, that it's time to surrender. Eventually, the individual gives up control of his or her own mind and spirit, and feels overwhelmed.

When someone seeks help from us, they have not yet fully given up. They may seem to be mired down in feelings of helplessness, but without any hope they would not have come to us. The goal of the therapist or of any helping person is to fan the embers of hope that remain glowing beneath the gloom.

The alternative to helplessness is a feeling of self-determination and mastery, the sense of taking control over one's own feelings and thoughts, and giving direction to one's life.

It is not the intensity of an emotion that makes it overwhelming or that induces emotional helplessness in us. People can experience enormous amounts of fear or sadness without collapsing in helplessness. It is the giving up, the sense of hopelessness in the face of the emotion, that makes it so debilitating. When a feeling of helplessness is building up inside someone over time, he or she may finally lose control in reaction to a seemingly slight frustration.

Blunting ourselves with drugs is not the answer to overwhelming emotions. Intense emotions should be welcomed. Emotions are the vital signs of life. We need and should want them to be strong. We also need our brains and minds to be functioning at their best, free of toxic drug effects. That allows us to use our intelligence and understanding to the fullest.

One of my colleagues, psychiatrist Joe Tarantolo, believes that medications have their effect by "taking the edge off the clarity of thinking," hence promoting confusion rather than mental acuity. Tarantolo asks his clients,[1] "At a time like this when you're in crisis, don't you want to be able to think as clearly as you can?" Thinking clearly is one of the hallmarks of taking charge of oneself instead of caving in to helplessness.

---

[1] Although he is a physician, Tarantolo believes that the term *client* is more empowering than *patient*.

Tarantolo points out that at crucial moments, when people verge on new discoveries about themselves, they can become frightened and take flight into confusion. Rather than admitting, "I'm frightened by what I'm discovering," they will feel and announce, "I'm confused." Instead of allowing themselves to remain confused, Tarantolo encourages his clients to face and to overcome their fears.

How can we encourage another person to remain confident in the face of overwhelming emotions? By being comfortable with that person's emotions and with the emotions they inspire in us. This is the key to the maintenance of our healing presence: our comfort with the other's emotions and the emotions that become aroused in us. As already suggested in discussing emotional contagion, when we turn to drastic measures in dealing with another person's feelings, it reflects our personal inability to handle what's being stirred up inside ourselves.

Of all the arts that helping persons need to practice, being comfortable with the emotions that others arouse in us is among the most important. This is true of therapists, teachers, parents, and friends.

Of all the ways in which we fail to help others, overreacting to their emotions is at the very top of the list. A distressed situation can be transformed into one that is healing once the therapist, parent, or teacher realizes the need to calmly accept the other person's emotions.

Being comfortable with intense emotions, including anger aimed at us, requires practice. How to practice it is probably as varied as the imagination. Among other things, I sometimes remind myself that my mere presence will be healing if I can remain comfortable with myself. That way I am less motivated to take retaliatory action or to say something punitive or suppressive.

Often I reassure myself I don't have to say anything at all, that I need only to listen carefully with genuine interest. Sometimes I have to remind myself that the other person's feelings, however intense or seemingly irrational, must be treasured as profound expressions of their experience of life. Above all else, I try to welcome the feelings as a window to the person's soul.

In facing frightening feelings within the other person and ourselves, we can remind ourselves that no one person, including a therapist, bears ultimate responsibility for anyone else's feelings or for anyone else's healing. This observation should never be turned into an excuse for giving up or for rejecting the other person. While we're not responsible for the other person's "cure," we are responsible for providing that person the best opportunity for healing. The client, of course, remains ultimately responsible for his or her own feelings.

Because of my books, many people call or write to me with the idea in mind that I am their "last resort." This is a very precarious way to start any kind of relationship, including therapy. It implies that the helper has more to do with the outcome than the person being helped. Besides, there are always people on earth other than us who may step forward to make healing contact. Many of them will probably be more effective than we are. Within this realistic perspective—that there are no great, indispensable, or last-resort therapists—a helper can be more fully present for the other person, lending his or her efforts to the creation of a genuinely therapeutic environment.

If we can remain entirely comfortable with others, despite their feelings of abject failure and doom, then they too may become more comfortable with themselves. They may conclude that all is not lost.

"I told you how bad it was and it didn't seem to faze you," my client tells me. I've succeeded, at that point at least, in maintaining a healing presence.

We need to find whatever method suits us for remaining comfortable in the face of intense and seemingly overwhelming emotions. Some people pray. Some people can hear music in their head (something I cannot do) and find peace in this. Others can see calming pictures in their mind's eye. Some people meditate. I silently remind myself that a loving attitude lies at the heart of being helpful. At the same time, I let myself see that the room and everything around us is potentially invested with healing aura— the grandeur of the human spirit.

Notice once again that being helpful to others is inseparable from being helpful to oneself. As we find confidence and comfort within ourselves, we will spontaneously provide it to others. And notice again the importance of our state of being. There are specific, useful techniques to be applied in formal therapy—self-defeating styles to be discovered, self-hating thoughts to be changed, wisdom to be shared, memories to be discovered, experiences to be recounted, emotions to be expressed. But in regard to another person's feelings of emotional overwhelm, our subjective state of being—our healing presence—remains crucial.

This chapter began with the basic truth that we are born into fear and helplessness and that this potential follows us through sickness and health, from infancy to old age. I mentioned how an infant becomes emotionally helpless when it is abandoned—when it loses nurture and love. In my experience, this is the root of most overwhelming helplessness—that we feel hopelessly cut off from human support at a moment when we cannot handle life alone.

Almost any human being can become "crazy." if placed in solitary confinement with no hope of human contact, if isolated too long on a life raft, or subjected to very extreme sensory deprivation. Successful techniques for demoralizing prisoners always rely on isolating them emotionally from each other. We need input from the world, but most importantly we need connectedness to other people or to some other aspect of life, from a treasured pet to nature or to ethical or religious ideals.

Psychosis is loosely defined as loss of contact with reality. But what reality? Usually it is a loss of *human* reality—of any sense of safe or secure connection or bonding with other people or other meaningful aspects of life. The deluded person who believes that he or she is controlled by an FBI computer is symbolically expressing a sense of being controlled by threatening human forces. To get into such a dreadful state, he or she must have first felt manipulated and controlled by other people. The reality of this suffering in regard to other people is so crushing that it is transformed into a metaphor of being oppressed by physical forces, such as government computers.

From sheer imagination, people find endless ways of creating or recreating missing human connections. These efforts often produce the "symptoms" of mental disorder. A man is obsessed with "love" for a woman whom he has never met. Despite the fact she's never heard of him, he finds imaginary signs that she secretly returns his love. Who else would be calling and hanging up? Who else would have thrown his newspaper from the sidewalk onto the porch? Who else would have given him that soothing touch in his dream? In real life, he is withdrawn from everyone. He creates a world of unreal connections where no real ones exist.

A woman hears voices telling her she is bad. They nag and abuse her. It turns out to be the voice of her mother. Lacking a loving relationship with her mother or any other childhood caregiver, her life has become dominated by her mother's communications of aggravation with her. This meager, miserable connection provides her only form of bonding.

Studies have shown that a childhood of neglect and weak bonding can be healed to a great extent by the presence of one loving adult somewhere along the way. Such is the nurturing power that each of us possesses in regard to others.

To be a loving person, one must have confidence in one's ability to love. This returns us once more to the state of being—the healing presence—of the person who wishes to be helpful. It should be a loving presence. In essence, we should be glad for the other's existence, we should take joy in our awareness of the other, however much he or she is suffering. The welcome we offer to another in pain is the most spiritually healing power we have.

Our capacity to comfort—our healing presence—consists, on the one hand, of not giving in to induced suffering or to the contagion of emotional helplessness. On the other, it consists of staying in touch with ourselves as loving beings and with others as treasures to be welcomed into our healing presence.

Remember my definition of love: joyful awareness. When we are joyfully aware of people, our feelings for them seem bathed in reverence. We recognize the sacred inviolability of their lives. We welcome their thoughts and feelings, however self-destructive or frightening, and nurture them in a caring aura.

Once again, I am not talking about a way of doing things. Psychological and spiritual healing is rarely about specific actions. It is about a way of being—being both aware and joyful at the same time. That is the essence of creating a healing presence.

Love can motivate us to do specific things, such as giving our time and energy in lifelong devotion to people, nature, justice, or God. But to be loving is first and foremost a spiritual state. It may encourage certain ways of approaching people, but it does not in itself require us to do anything. Love can be unconditional because it has more to do with our own inner state than with the "object" of our love, whether it be a friend or a pet, a season or a sunset, a principle or an ideal.

Notice once again that my definition of love does not include suffering. Loss of love may cause us to suffer. Jealousy in a loving relationship may ruin both our inner state and the relationship. Our capacity to empathize with the suffering of others may also at times bring us sorrow. But none of this is the essence of love. We confuse suffering with love because we so often become emotionally upset and overwhelmed in the context of what seems like a loving relationship.

To feel loving is in fact to feel empowered—to feel in control of one's own spiritual state. To feel loving is to feel glad to be alive.

How can we remain joyful in the presence of someone else's suffering—or even our own suffering? By recognizing that suffering is a sign of life, not death. By remaining glad that the other is alive. By remaining glad that we are alive. By remaining connected to each other.

If we can maintain this attitude of joyful awareness when in the presence of suffering human beings, we will maximize our capacity to heal ourselves and to heal them. In a way that makes little distinction between the benefits to ourselves and to others, we will become a healing person.

Most of us believe that, under some conditions, life makes it impossible to maintain a joyful, welcoming, or grateful attitude. But there is no way to define these limits for any specific person. Religious martyrs demonstrate that faith in God can inspire joy even in the face of torture and death. We admire anyone who can face chronic illness, death, or great losses with a loving attitude toward life and a welcoming attitude to other people.

Unlike some religious disciples, I do not think we have it in our power to "make every moment the happiest moment of our lives." I recently listened to that philosophy, as recorded from a workshop that was given by a Buddhist to a group of therapists. I very much respect the man who made the remarks and I've learned from his books. Yet the very concept smacks of separation and even isolation from others. How can it be our happiest moment when our child screams in pain? How can it be our happiest moment when we have learned of yet another epidemic, earthquake, or war? It's up to us to be as heroic, principled, and empathic as we can be—from moment to moment in our lives—and often that will promote our satisfaction and happiness. That's a far cry from focusing our attention on making each moment the happiest of our lives.

Most of us are heroic in one way or another in our lives. I have been impressed by the unsung everyday heroism of many people. My neighbor, Joe, for example, nursed his wife for years as she died inexorably from brain cancer. My client, Janet, overcame multiple prior breakdowns and psychiatric hospitalizations to become the successful mother of a large family. My friend, Joan, learned she had a fatal cancer and turned herself around from a defensive and hostile person to a loving wife and mother in her last years. Our former housekeeper, Mindy, overcame poverty and racism to be a responsible church leader, wife, parent, and worker. My friends, Sharon, Barbara, and Charles Anna transcended racism and sexism to shine as beacons of truth in their communities, professions, and personal lives. My wife's parents, Jean and Phil, could have retired into a complacent older age, but took increasing risks by standing up against those who pollute the environment of their midwestern state and hometown. Again, my wife's parents, middle-class white Presbyterians from America's heartland, responded with love to their own children's determination to build multiracial, multireligious "rainbow" families.

Some of us are heroic about one thing, but not about another. One person's marvelous challenge is another's undoing; one person's undoing is another person's revitalizing challenge.

I have been both mystified and inspired by this phenomenon among my clients over the years: What threatens one person to the core hardly scratches the surface of another, and vice versa. I have noticed the same thing in regard to everyone I know. We each have our "Achilles' heel" as well as our strengths. The strengths and weaknesses, however, vary drastically from person to person. While we are all born into fear and helplessness, and struggle with it all of our lives, we differ vastly in what activates these feelings within us.

Since being heroic and being intimidated are so subjective, why not assume that the people we are trying to help can handle what life has presented to them? If we are going to be helpful, in most cases we should begin by assuming that the persons we are helping can master themselves and their situation. We should recognize and accept their feelings of fear and helplessness without confirming that they must remain incapacitated by their problems.

As already emphasized on several occasions, we should not deny our own inadequacies or exaggerate our abilities. Charismatic flawlessness is incompatible with self-insight and empathy. There are times when, due to our own limitations, we cannot maintain a spiritual state that's consistent with understanding, honoring, treasuring, and empowering the other person. This can happen in professional relationships as well as in everyday life.

When we feel we can no longer be helpful to other people, we should—without blaming it on them—direct them toward other help. In both personal and professional relationships, this should be done without rejection or abandonment. That we cannot maintain our own spiritual composure is our problem, not theirs. Even if dozens of others have also failed to be helpful to a particular person, there may be someone right around the corner who is able and prepared to offer help.

In psychiatry, the reverse attitude is almost always taken. If the person seeking help remains depressed or anxious despite the psychiatrist's best effort to provide psychotherapy, the psychiatrist will almost invariably recommend drugs. The assumption is that "talking therapy didn't work" rather than "my talking therapy wasn't helpful to this person." If several drugs fail to bring about improvement, the doctor may recommend hospitalization and shock treatment. Instead, the psychiatrist should have viewed himself or herself, rather than the other person, as the probable cause of the failure in therapy. The patient should have been directed toward someone else.

Finding and maintaining a relationship with a professional helper can be fraught with difficulty. It can require considerable "shopping around" to find the right person for you. Here's one place where chemistry does count—the chemistry of the soul rather than the chemistry of pharmaceuticals.

For a number of reasons, we may find ourselves unable to maintain a healing presence with another person or to remain helpful to them. Perhaps they remind us of people who have caused us pain earlier in our lives. Their difficulties may stir up our own unresolved problems. Their suffering may seem unbearable to us. By temperament we may be ill-equipped to understand this particular person. The person's behavior, which threatens harm toward himself or others, may put us in too much jeopardy. Whatever the reasons—and often we cannot identify them—we should accept our own limitations as helping persons. We cannot be all things to all people. We can only offer our own particular way of being helpful.

Nothing I have said should ever be used as an excuse for rejecting or abandoning someone who has come to us seeking help. There are other ways to go about admitting our own limitations. We can suggest alternative therapists as a source of consultation and open the door for our client to turn to them instead of us. We can suggest different therapeutic approaches, such as a group or seminar, where new contacts may be made. We can make clear that we think the client needs something more, without withdrawing our support in the process. In the meantime, it remains the therapist's solemn duty to find within himself or herself the resources to be helpful to this person.

Within psychiatry, a great deal of abuse is heaped on patients because individual psychiatrists or psychotherapists cannot accept their own emotional, spiritual, or therapeutic limitations. There are probably others, but I know only one psychotherapist, my friend Jeffrey Masson, who became fully trained and then admitted he wasn't good at it. Think of the courage involved in a decision—to discard years of professional training because we realize we're not good at it. Also, think about the tens of thousands of other therapists who never found the courage to make a similar admission to themselves. When a patient is drugged or shocked by a psychiatrist, it usually says more about the doctor's spiritual failure than about the "diagnosis" of the patient (see also chapter 17).

To be a helping person we must continually revive an empathic, loving spiritual attitude toward ourselves and others. To do this, we must be comfortable with whatever emotions we face in others, including the emotions that become aroused in us.

We must resist succumbing to emotional helplessness in the face of the suffering in others. We must refuse to push drastic measures when we are seemingly unable to help. We must make other people and resources available when we ourselves seem unable to help. We must remain loving—joyfully aware and welcoming—in regard to ourselves and others, even during extreme stress. In short, we must remain glad that we are all alive.

There is a basic truth about human life that provides direction during times of emotional overwhelm: All of us are born into a condition of fear and helplessness, and throughout our adult lives, we continue to need other people to help overcome it. While working together, both the healer and the person being healed are likely to struggle with fear and helplessness. The creation of healing presence and healing aura requires recognition of this truth and willingness to reach out in the face of fear and helplessness to offer the security, comfort, and joy of genuine human caring.

How to Help in Extreme Emotional Crises

9

When do our own feelings get in the way of helping? What's wrong with treating emotional crises as emergencies? How can we turn crises into creative opportunities?

Mel found his girlfriend, Mary, in bed with his best friend. It was the most humiliating experience of life. He was "reduced to nothing"—not by his girlfriend, but by his best friend.

Mel fled back to his own apartment, threw himself down on his bed, and howled. A wave of humiliation rolled over him. There was only one solution: Kill his best friend. He loaded his pistol, got into his car, and took off. On the way, Mel decided to stop by his psychologist's office. As it turned out, Sean was available.

The nature of Mel's emergency was apparent: a monstrous attack of humiliation. He felt rendered into such "a nothing"—such an impotent nonentity—that only by violence against the perpetrator could he redeem himself. Sean knew that Mel worked part-time as a security guard while going to school. Sean could guess what was causing the bulge beneath Mel's jacket at the hip.

Mel had first come to see Sean several months earlier, at Mary's request, to deal with his inability to make a commitment to her. On occasion she joined him in his sessions to talk about their relationship, and it was apparent they were very much in love. Sean liked them both and Mel was a special treat. He had a diamond-in-the-rough quality that was refreshing in its difference from most of the sophisticated people in Sean's practice. Mel in turn couldn't believe he "got along so well with a shrink."

Now, in a torrent of words, Mel spilled out the awful situation. Murder seemed like the only way out. Sean, meanwhile, was walking a thin line. If Mel remained a threat to someone else, Sean was bound by ethics and by law to take action to warn the intended victim.

When Mel finished telling Sean the story, the psychologist let out an enormous sigh. Something was being stirred up in him.

"Why do you think Mary did it?' Sean asked.

Mel got very silent. He didn't want to admit that Mary had anything to do with it.

"What happened between you two?" Sean asked.

"Oh, you know," he said sheepishly.

"Not *that* again?" Sean said.

"Yeah, that."

"You started fooling around with that girl at the office again?" Sean realized that his tone seemed too sharp.

Mel nodded even more sheepishly. "I don't know why I do it. I love Mary so damn much. You know, Sean, you and I have talked it to death already. I just get scared. And so I stayed out late again and Mary guessed. I couldn't lie to her."

Sean was tempted to say "I told you so," but he didn't. Sean even wanted to say, "I don't blame you for wanting to kill that guy," but he held back. Irrational stuff swirled through the therapist's mind. Then he felt angry at Mel. He wanted to bawl out his client for threatening to kill another person, for not facing his own issues, for not making better use of therapy, and so on.

Sean realized that he was reacting irrationally to Mel. Sean kept his mouth shut and made up his mind to work harder to stay in touch with what Mel was feeling. He remembered something about himself: his tendency to get judgmental when the other person was doing something he himself had done or wanted to do. He was really judging himself.

Sean was not only feeling initially judgmental toward Mel, he was scared about the consequences. As Mel continued talking, a horrible vision of Mel killing someone crossed Sean's imagination. If he couldn't help his client overcome his murderous impulses, what was he going to do? Suppose Mel fled from his office with the gun still in his possession? Sean would have to call the police. It was his moral and legal duty to protect the potential victim but it might be too late to stop Mel. And calling the police could harm Mel's life and probably ruin any hope of Mel accepting future help from any therapist.

"I feel all confused," Mel protested.

Sean and Mel were both silent and then Sean realized what was happening. Sean had been through the same thing himself—more than once. Twice in fact, when he was much younger. Twice friends had seemingly betrayed him with women in his life. It was unbearable to remember.

"Mel, I know what you're feeling. Like the worst thing that could ever happen to you in your whole life. I really understand how badly you want to kill him."

"Sean, I have to kill him. It's got to be me or him."

"I understand," Sean said and wiped a tear away.

"You understand?" Mel said with doubt. He tended to idealize Sean as a miraculously loving, nonviolent man. This had to do with how angry he often felt. By contrast, Sean seemed to him like a saint. It also had to do with how much Sean liked him. Sean was the only significant man in his life who ever treated him with kindness and affection.

"Oh, yeah, I understand," Sean said grimly.

"Well, nothing like this ever happened to you," Mel insisted.

Sean held up his hand and raised two fingers. It had the odd effect of looking like a victory sign when it symbolized ultimate humiliation.

"Twice. Your best friend with your girlfriend—twice?" he said with dismay.

"My two best friends, two different women I was dating," Sean said. "I was about your age at the time."

"You should have killed both of them."

Knowing how many men tend to think, Sean realized that Mel was talking about killing the other men and not the women. Mel wanted to believe that men remained responsible for these situations. It felt too vulnerable to imagine a woman, like Mary, making the choice.

"You didn't, did you?" Mel said the obvious.

Sean shook his head and sighed again. "I guess I wouldn't be here, if I had."

The images from those many years ago were flooding back to Sean. He felt very young and vulnerable again.

"Both times—it was just about the worst experience of my life," Sean confessed to him.

Mel nodded vigorously to show his agreement.

"It does make you feel like you're nothing," Sean said.

"Like your friend is just laughing up his sleeve. He screws your girl and screws you, too," Mel explained. "But twice, it happened to you twice? Two different guys?"

"Yep. I was a slow learner."

"Did you get a gun?"

"I wanted to use my bare hands. It was just a feeling. I never threatened anyone."

"I can't believe anybody would do that to you. I mean, who could treat you like you were nothing?"

"It's not about who we are," Sean said, knowing that wouldn't at first make much sense to Mel.

"But you let them get away with it?"

"Well, you know, it's not really about us—about me or you," Sean said.

"It sure is. Who the hell else could it be about?"

"It's about their own stuff. Would *you* do that to a friend of yours—even if you fell in love with his girlfriend?"

"Never. Never. I'd sit down with my buddy, maybe with both of them. I'd say, look what's happened. I'm falling in love with Mary."

Mary's name had slipped out. Mel started to cry over being in love with her.

"But he's not in love with her. He was doing it to get at me. It's like my worst nightmare," Mel started to cry again. His face was crimson with humiliation. It was the first time he had ever shown so much feeling.

Sean got up, sat on the hassock, and hugged him. It was a short, awkward hug, typical of many guys.

"I just don't know what to do," Mel said. "I feel so used. I always knew that SOB was competing with me, trying to one-up me. I mean, he's fun, we do a lot of stuff together, we go back a long way, but I should have figured he'd do something like this."

"If I were you, I'd get a new best friend and I'd treat Mary better."

"Treat Mary better—after this?"

"That's what I had to learn, anyway," Sean confessed. "The truth is, Mel, I wasn't giving either of the women what they needed. I wasn't ready to commit myself to them. I'm not even sure I really loved them. Maybe that's why they got involved with my friends."

"You think, after all this, I should admit I love her? I mean, I do love her. You know that. I mean, I should tell her I'll be faithful to her forever?"

"Well, I think it's about time, don't you?" Sean grinned. "You've been working on it in therapy for 6 months!"

He broke out laughing. "You mean, I'm supposed to give you the gun, go find Mary, forgive her, tell her I'm sorry and I want her back?"

Sean nodded, glad his client was the first one to bring up the gun.

"I want to kill him," he protested, almost whining, the way a child does when he knows he's wrong and has to give up on something. "Killing him doesn't make a lot of sense, does it?"

"It makes a lot of *emotional* sense, Mel, or you wouldn't feel it so strongly. It's just not *rational* or *good* sense. You're worth more than that. So's Mary."

"I won't do it," he sighed.

"I'm glad to hear that. I'd hate to lose you. It would break my heart. It would destroy Mary." Sean decided to be even more honest. "It would mess up my life pretty bad, too, personally and professionally."

"Yeah, I thought about you," Mel said. Then with embarrassment, "I came by here to save you—from me. I figured if I killed him you'd get blamed. I couldn't let that happen, not to you, Sean."

"It's like that when you care about people," Sean confirmed. "You end up saving yourself because you don't want to hurt the people you care about."

"It would kill Mary, too. I mean, emotionally kill her, wouldn't it? She'd blame herself for everything, wouldn't she?"

"Murder scars everyone," Sean agreed, "including those who survive."

Mel nodded that he understood.

"So does suicide, Mel," Sean suggested.

Although Mel hadn't hinted at suicide. Sean knew that it often went along with murder. First the pent-up violence is turned on someone else, then on oneself.

"Yeah, suicide. It crossed my mind. You know me too well," he managed to laugh.

Sean went on, "The people left behind are changed forever. Mary would have blamed herself and she would have missed you, too."

"Maybe I wanted to get even with her," he told himself thoughtfully.

Sean and Mel were both quiet for a while. Sean was savoring the importance of the relationship and the importance of the lives of all the people involved.

"You saved that guy's life, Sean. Mine, too. Mary's, too, I guess."

The two men sat quietly again. Then they talked some about how Mel could approach Mary. He would have to take responsibility for repeatedly hurting her. There was a chance she wouldn't even want him back. It was a frightening situation for Mel.

"Man, I owe you a lot, my life, really," he said. His code of conduct made him indebted to Sean for his life.

"Mel, remember that time you were on guard duty—the time you broke up that attempted rape in the parking lot?"

"Yeah, of course I remember. I still got a scar from it."

"You saved that woman from the worst humiliation in her life and maybe even saved her life. And you risked your life for her."

He shrugged, "Maybe so."

"Did that woman 'owe' you?"

"Nope. It was my job. Besides, it's what any man should have done. It makes me sick when guys do that to women."

"You don't owe me, either, Mel. It's my job . . . and I love you, Mel, and I sure am glad you're not going to kill anyone."

Mel took the revolver out of his belt.

"I'm not going to do anything stupid anymore, but *you* would feel better if I left the gun with you for a few days, wouldn't you?"

"I sure would," Sean confirmed.

Mel emptied out the bullets, separated the cylinder from the gun, put the cylinder back in his pocket, and left the disabled pistol on the table.

Mel was too responsible to leave Sean with a working pistol to worry about.

They talked for a while longer about humiliation and how it could drive people to want to kill. Sean wanted his client to know that he wasn't alone in his feelings—that almost all murderous feelings were driven by humiliation.

Mel said, "You know how much you're always asking me to talk more about my childhood?"

"Yeah," Sean acknowledged. "I know how you hate to do it."

"I'm always telling you that childhood stuff is garbage," he reminded Sean. "I'm always saying I don't want to make excuses because of something that happened to me when I was 10."

"You tell me that all the time," Sean smiled.

"But it's like you say. Why throw my life away—and Mary's too—just to prove some guy can't put one over on me? It's like being a kid all over again. Watching my father beating on my mother, trying to force himself on her. He's drunk and she's trying to get out from under him."

It wasn't the first time this scene from his childhood had come up. It summed up the repeated abuse he and his mother had endured from his father, years of it, until his father died of alcoholism. His father's assault on his mother was the most dreadful memory from his childhood. Now it was compressed into his most dreadful experience in adulthood.

"I wanted to kill him, too," he said of his father.

Mel began to cry again.

"Well, the hell with them both. I'm not wasting my life over screwed-up guys, my father, my friend, or anybody."

At the end of their meeting, they shook hands warmly, hugged and then Mel left.

Sean made a mental note to talk more about Mel's feelings toward his friend and his father. Mel loved his friend and maybe his father, too. But neither of them was trustworthy. Mel and Sean would have to talk about men caring about each other, the threats, the dangers, and the need to select better friends.

It began to dawn on Sean that Mel's fear of commitment to a woman might have more to do with men than with women. Mel had watched his revered mother suffer continued abuse. He loved but couldn't protect her. Now he loved Mary and feared he couldn't protect the relationship. Fear and helplessness stimulated by men like his father and his friend made him feel too vulnerable to risk loving Mary. But that conversation was for another day when the crisis was past and Mel was feeling less vulnerable.

Sean remembered how long it took himself to recover from feeling so betrayed by his friends. Men in modern society are afraid of intimacy with each other, often for real reasons. They have been taught to compete with each other—to triumph over each other. To become a helping person with other men requires understanding the competitiveness and personally leaving it behind.

Sean decided to call Mel that evening to "say hello." He wanted to make sure his client felt secure about their relationship. Sean also wanted to reaffirm that he would be glad to see him additional times in the coming weeks at a reduced rate.

Some therapists might disagree with providing occasional sessions for free or at a reduced price. It can work well, first, by providing needed help at difficult times and, second, by strengthening the healing relationship.

As in almost every psychological emergency, this one ended up shedding new and refreshing light on Mel's inner struggles. He was going to come through it with increased understanding of himself. Sean had also done some new thinking about himself.

Emergencies are opportunities. If they don't scare us into doing something drastic, if we can maintain our healing presence, they are the most opportune time for self-insight, growth, and bonding.

Sean called Mel at his apartment that night to let him know he was thinking about him. Mary answered the phone. She sounded very happy. She told Sean that Mel, from the heart, had promised to be faithful. For the first time ever, he had cried with her, too. He had asked her to marry him.

Some of Sean's approach during Mel's emergency was informed by being a professional therapist. Without his clinical experience, Sean might not have understood how Mel's feelings of humiliation were driving him to violence. Sean also might not have brought out the link between Mel's childhood experiences and his current emotional crisis. Sean's experience made him aware of the danger of the potential for suicide.

These insights were probably not the key elements in helping Mel through his anguish and rage, however. More important was their relationship, the healing aura they generated together. Mel's courage and confidence in dealing with Sean helped to create the beneficial atmosphere, and so did Sean's willingness to examine himself in the interest of being more empathic and available. Mel and Sean care about each other. That mutual affection made it hard for Mel to hang on to murderous impulses or to throw his life away out of pride and humiliation.

The experience with Mel illustrates a key principle in handling extreme emotions: Find something in yourself that resonates with the emotions of the other person, and then accept that aspect of yourself and the other person. Sean verbalized with Mel their common experiences. Often, however, that's not necessary or even appropriate. What matters most is being comfortable and empathic with the other person's extreme or irrational feelings.

As Sean's work with Mel illustrated, there's more to helping people than being empathic. Sometimes it requires special training, experience, knowledge, or wisdom. But being empathic—developing a healing presence—is the starting point. It's not only the most essential ingredient in helping, it's an absolutely necessary one. Without empathy, there can be no genuine help.

There's another key principle in handling extreme emotional emergencies, one that always causes initial skepticism when I announce it during workshops for professionals. Eventually it brings smiles of recognition. Those of us who work well with "emergencies"—and even enjoy them—are acting on this unstated principle. It helps to verbalize it. The principle is this: Never treat an emotional "emergency" as if it is an emergency.

Instead, make the most of the situation as an opportunity for deeper contact with the other person and with ourselves as well.

Crises are like that; they open us up to more real communication. Assume that the situation can be handled—that the crisis can become a manageable and even positive opportunity for the person we are trying to help. Then pitch in to understand how and why the other person feels doomed or feels compelled to act destructively.

The temptation is to do something to the other person: to take a strong stand about his or her behavior, to call the police, to suggest drugs or a mental hospital. In Mel's case, Sean rejected doing something to him. Instead, Sean did something to himself. He let himself resonate with Mel's feelings of overwhelming humiliation without giving in to them. Sean found the source of similar feelings within himself, used it to understand his situation, and shared his wisdom with him.

Sometimes we may feel hard pressed to find a personal experience of our own that resembles or resonates with that of the person we are trying to help. Obviously, not everyone would have such a similar personal experience as Sean to draw on in helping Mel. But if we're in touch with ourselves, we will be aware of horrible humiliations in our own life.

All of us have felt enough emotional pain in our own lives to identify with the suffering of others. All of us have been sufficiently unreasonable to feel sympathy with the irrationality of others. All of us have been tempted enough by irresponsibility to understand that same impulse in others. By being honest with ourselves, we can remain open to others.

Because Sean did not leap into the situation with Mel as if it were an emergency, Sean did not begin by confronting Mel's possession of the gun. Sean figured if Mel could develop another perspective—that he wasn't the victim of a disaster requiring a violent solution—the rest would follow.

If we can act as if an emotional crisis isn't an emergency, then we are likely to handle the crisis with relative ease. When feeling hopelessly overwhelmed, people don't need us to confirm their helplessness for them by making an emergency intervention. They need us to take their problem in stride while maintaining our healing presence. This is true if we're in the role of counselor, therapist, teacher, minister, parent, or friend. The worst approach is to agree there's an emergency going on. That will only confirm the other person's worst fears.

Emergencies should be handled with the expectation that they will become exceedingly interesting experiences—marvelous opportunities to see into another person's heart, while seeing into one's own as well. What starts out for everyone as an unwanted crisis can turn into something for which we all feel grateful. Often these crises lead to a new level of bonding. As a helping person, turning an emergency into an opportunity for growth is one of the most fulfilling experiences we can have.

The ultimate goal in dealing with an emotional or spiritual emergency is to empower the other person—to help that individual discover that life can be handled and, even better, that life is an exciting challenge. An emergency can become a transforming experience. The individual confronts his or her worst fears and most extreme tendencies toward helplessness and learns that they can be turned into spiritually uplifting challenges.

Sometimes clients find it useful to develop a personal mantra for themselves to repeat when they verge on losing control of themselves. It can be especially useful to remind oneself, in effect, "I'm not a small child anymore. I'm not threatened by huge and powerful adults. I'm grown up and can handle whatever comes along."

Although few people realize it, even the most threatening real-life events, such as potentially fatal diseases or the loss of a loved one, gain much of their power over us by restimulating childhood trauma. They make us feel once again like helpless children. For example, a child who feels chronically threatened by adults may grow into an adult who feels distrustful and fearful of people. If we identify our overwhelming childhood experiences and become comfortable with them, we can remain more rational and loving in the face of adult stresses.

People can transform themselves from feeling overwhelmed to feeling empowered if we approach them with dignity, empathy, and a determination not to overreact. As always when trying to be helpful to people, the hardest and most important work requires making sure that our own spiritual state reflects the heart of being helpful. We must first tend to our own healing presence.

Trying to help people in emotional crises will stir up our own most painful past experiences and our underlying feelings of fear and helplessness. To turn crises into creative opportunities, we must first become comfortable with our own reactions. Especially, we must resist the temptation to react to crises as if they are emergencies. If we prematurely turn to drastic interventions, we escalate the other person's worst fears. Emotional crises are opportunities to foster understanding and to strengthen bonding. They enable us to help the individual in identifying his or her self-defeating approaches and to assist in finding more creative ones.

Remember that we are all born into fear and helplessness. This becomes obvious in emotional emergencies. When overcome in a crisis, we have been thrust back in time to feeling like a terrified, lonely, helpless child with nowhere to turn. It's useful to acknowledge this fear and helplessness to ourselves—not to succumb to it but to subject it to the healing light of consciousness. Then we can avoid acting on these self-destructive impulses. Instead, we can ameliorate the crisis through our calming, healing presence.

Creation of Healing Aura in Families   **10**

Why is couples or family therapy especially helpful? How can we teach families to imbue their lives with love? Why is "improved communication" not in itself enough? What lessons can we learn from therapy about improving our family lives?

Human beings are social creatures. We are made of our experiences with each other. With or without professional therapy, nothing helps an individual grow more than a loving, supportive family, and nothing can hold a person back as much as destructive family relationships. I have seen husbands and wives transform each other's lives for the better. I have also witnessed them ruin each other's lives.

Improving family life too often gets reduced to "improving communication." Communication is of course important—but communication about what? And communication based on what? Without an underlying set of principles, such as love and respect for autonomy, communication is likely to remain superficial and unsatisfying. Family life should be bathed in love.

John is a devout man who owns a well-known business in the city and tithes a substantial sum to his church each year. He is treasurer of his church and spends much of his time fund-raising. His life is devoted to community and to God.

John was reluctant to come to therapy, in part because it seemed to reflect poorly on his "position in the community." He also believed that his religion, and not psychotherapy, should provide him solace and guidance. His wife, Sheila, insisted that they consult me. She loved John very much and began by describing how God had inspired their getting together. Now she could no longer endure the isolation she felt. She herself had never been in therapy but was more welcoming of the process.

Sheila and John, like so many couples who arrive for therapy, were at each other's throats. She raged against him for failing to respond to any of her needs; he sat and suffered under her assault, occasionally glowering in a menacing fashion. He would use her more nasty remarks as justification for not trying to communicate with her. She felt driven to excessive accusations by his stony lack of responsiveness.

As I sat listening to Sheila's monologue, a litany of John's "emotional crimes" against her, I wondered how John could stand to remain in the same room. He sat impassively, but I knew he was suffering. As I watched John, the pillar of the community acting like a concrete pillar in front of his wife, I could understand the frustration and outrage that fueled her assault on him. After about half an hour, I interrupted and commented on how much pain they were inflicting on each other. They seemed relieved at my understanding of their individual suffering at each other's hands.

We worked on communication in the first session: how their tactics hurt each other and brought out the worst in each other. We set some ground rules about more respectful communication and about responding more directly to sincere questions.

As I tried to help them untangle their destructive ways of talking—and not talking—with each other, something else became apparent in the next several sessions. In trying to get closer to John, Sheila really was banging her head against a stone wall. She was trying to build a more intimate partnership with John; he was trying to fend it off so that he could get back to work. With their aims wholly at odds with each other, it was no wonder their communications fell on deaf ears.

Despite the enormous energy he put into his spiritual life, John felt spiritually lost. He was not only unable to talk to his wife, he was unable to talk to God. He was becoming an empty fortress.

I don't speak in spiritual terms with my clients unless they have a desire for it. I'm not Christian, so I didn't share or fully understand John and Sheila's Protestant religion; but I had a sense of shared values with them. When people believe in God, as many of my clients do, love for each other can bring them nearer to God and love for God can bring them nearer to each other. I believe that love between people is a spiritual bond connecting us not only to our loved ones but to humanity, to nature, to all that we can treasure about life.

After another session, it became apparent that their difficulties in communication went beyond style. They had to do with content—with opposing goals. I began to talk with John about his underlying values while his wife beamed approval of the new direction we were taking. John readily admitted that his life seemed like a tragic, futile effort to find spiritual fulfillment. He had been depressed all of his life and, as it turned out, had sought psychiatric help on numerous occasions. He was no hypocrite—he knew that he worked so hard partly because he felt so empty—but he didn't know what to do about it.

I asked John what he felt about the presence of God in his marriage. He grew embarrassed, even shy, as if he'd never been asked before. Of course, the topic had come up in innumerable workshops and sermons; but having it come up in therapy was another matter. It became more real, more personal, more urgent.

John confessed, "When I first met Sheila, I felt God's hand in it. I could almost hear Him voicing approval. . . . I know in my head that marriage is meant as partnership that brings us closer to God. I know there's a connection between a personal relationship with my wife and my personal relationship with God. I know that I've never been able to feel close to any woman. I know I've never been able to feel close to God. I know all of this in my head but not in my heart."

"John," Sheila was nearly overcome with feeling, "I've never heard you talk this way! Why don't you talk with me about these things?"

I held up my hand to signal she was being too accusatory when he was being vulnerable. She nodded that she understood.

John said to her, "Men aren't supposed to talk this way about their wives." Marveling over the thought, he said "I've never talked this way with another man—about the importance of our wives."

"Why not?" she asked, but he could only shrug in response.

"It's hard for men," I said to both of them, ". . . hard for us to admit how much we need our wives." I paused and asked John, "Have you ever made a woman—any woman—the top priority in your life?"

"It's been impossible," he blurted out. Turning to his wife, he said, "I watch our fighting like a man on a mountaintop looking down on it. I see how much you need me and I just can't respond. I can't come off the mountain. I see that I'm breaking your heart, but there's nothing inside to give."

We talked for a while longer and I said, "I don't know how you feel about it, John, but personally I don't feel it's wrong for a man to feel incomplete without his wife."

"Oh, it sounds so weak, so needy," he said. But his words seemed more accusing toward himself than toward me. He told his wife, "It's like I'm supposed to admit that I couldn't live without you."

"I can't live without you," she said. "I feel like I'm dying inside when I don't have you." She said to me, "Peter, it's so scary to hear it all come out—John on that mountaintop all by himself—but it feels good to have it out in the open."

"It's scary to me," John admitted, "this whole thing about needing anyone, making anyone more important than everything else."

"You don't even want to make God that important?" I wondered aloud.

He shook his head in agreement. "No, not even God."

"John," I explained, "I know what you mean about sounding needy and weak. Most of my life, I fought against those feelings. Then it began to dawn on me: I had to accept how much I need a loved one, how much I need people, and how much I need God. I didn't like any of it. It embarrassed me. It made me feel weak. It made me feel irrational."

"You don't look needy," he said, wondering if his eyes were deceiving him.

"I don't feel needy at this moment, John, because I've accepted how needy I am. I'm so open with myself about being needy that I can work to get my needs fulfilled."

"It makes sense," he said without enthusiasm, as if it were beyond his capacity.

"How long have you been depressed, John?"

"As long as I can remember," he said.

"Well, it doesn't sound like you have much to lose," I gently teased him. "Why not admit you're needy? Why not admit you're weak? Isn't that what it's all about—needing God, needing people, needing love. Isn't that the starting point of our spiritual life?"

"It's what my religion teaches," John said. "It's what I've taught other people. But I've never seen myself so clearly."

John thought quietly for a few minutes. Sheila remained silent, taking a renewed interest in listening rather than in talking. She felt hopeful that John would communicate something meaningful.

John began again, "I've been trying to make my religion work without needing God. I've been trying to make my marriage work without needing Sheila. No wonder I'm so depressed."

John looked at Sheila with tears streaming down his face. "I love you," he said, "But I'm so damn frightened."

We had work ahead of us. Their ways of communicating with each other required improvement. Sheila most certainly would have her own underlying issues. John would have to struggle with the model that his father had provided of a man who didn't need anyone. But by the end of the session, they were able to renew their marriage. John, for the first time, verbally committed himself to making their relationship the center of his spiritual life.

John was a mature, very responsible, highly successful man, but much of his problem was rooted in his childhood. In couples therapy, the drama of his childhood was reenacted, as he sought to find a way out of the isolation of his childhood. He was still emulating his father's example that had been reinforced by our society with its values of male domination and control. John's model of the strong male standing in splendid isolation made it impossible for him to open his heart to anyone, including his wife and God.

Early family life is so formative that improvements in the parent–child relationship, even when the child has become an adult, can vastly increase the quality of life for everyone involved. If John's father had been alive, I might have suggested that John come in with him. If the two men could have opened up to each other, it might have transformed both their lives.

If a couple decides they can't love each other—that they cannot build a life immersed in love—that conclusion in itself can make the therapy worthwhile to the participants. They have come to grips with the limits of the relationship. It is up to them to decide what to do: whether to accommodate to each other in living a relatively loveless life or to seek more bonding for themselves in other relationships.

Although I believe that passionate love is worth searching for, there are often serious complications in breaking up an existing family. Sometimes one member is ill or dying, and the other feels an obligation born of personal commitment and years of sharing life together. Many people choose to stay together until their children are old enough to leave home. Often a husband or wife chooses to remain married out of economic considerations. There is no easy formula for making these decisions and they must be left up to each individual. A therapist should help people find their own solutions. To make enlightened choices, they need to understand love.

People not only need to love each other, they simply need each other. There is too much emphasis in our society on what might be called pseudoindependence—making believe we don't need or affect each other. I have also called it nondependence—the failure to relate disguised as independence. Therapists too often tell their clients, "No one can make you feel unhappy or make you feel happy. It has to come from within yourself." Nonsense. People have an extraordinary capacity to make each other miserable and to bring joy to each other. One of the keys to successful living is to learn how to surround oneself with loving, empowering, ethical people.

There is also too much emphasis on "getting along" in oppressive relationships. Grown children are often encouraged to "make up" with their parents, or to reach an accommodation, without the parents changing their abusive ways or learning to be more loving.

Because we are such social beings, family therapy can bring to light issues that remain hidden during individual therapy. A man may seem a model of patience and understanding when talking with his therapist, only to become short-tempered, hostile, and manipulative when his wife arrives with him for a session. A young boy who is intensely focused while working with me alone may become "hyperactive" the moment his parents enter the office. A woman may hide her alcoholism, a man may hide his sexual fears and difficulties, until a spouse discloses the secret in a couples session.

More subtle conflicts may quickly become apparent in family therapy. People withhold love, express disdain, and make threats in subtle fashions with the significant members of their lives. An arched eyebrow may mean, "I'll get you for that when we get home." A slight smile may mean, "You're being a jerk again." A frown may indicate, "I'm going to act depressed the entire weekend." In individual therapy without the husband or wife, these communication styles may never surface. In the presence of the spouse, they may rear up within the first seconds.

People who are very disturbed and injured, including those who carry the diagnosis of schizophrenia, often can benefit most from family therapy. Like everyone else, their way of being has been influenced by significant people during their formative years. In the case of especially impaired people, some of whom continue to live at home in a dependent fashion, ongoing family relationships can be critical to their healing. By helping families to develop less conflicted, more loving communication and relationships, we go to the heart of the problem of "schizophrenia"—alienation from other human beings and withdrawal into a private world of humiliation and anger.

Family therapy isn't always feasible or more effective than individual therapy. More than half of my clinical practice is with individuals. But family therapy has special advantages and, quite often, will work when other approaches have failed abysmally.

By the time they seek help, families are usually enmeshed in complex, subtle but devastating conflicts. In therapy, I point out each destructive communication and show how it perpetuates conflict and suffering. Like John and Sheila, each person almost always has a repetitive, compulsive, defensive style of communicating that does more harm than good. If the individuals are well motivated, awareness of these largely unconscious or reflexive patterns may be quickly appreciated. If more positive alternatives can be drawn to their attention, the participants may rapidly begin to work on changing their behavior. When the goal of a more rational and loving life together is made explicit, progress can proceed even more readily.

Working with couples and families often brings out the underlying suffering more directly than working with individuals. When a couple like John and Sheila try to communicate in more respectful, caring ways, they can become immediately aware of how much frustration and suffering lies beneath their attacks on each other.

When John comes down off his mountain, he is likely for a time to feel frightened by his new vulnerability. He may become temporarily more depressed as he realizes the depth of his unfulfilled needs. Similarly, when Sheila has to deal with a more "needy" and more loving John, she may discover her own problems in giving and accepting love. She may find that her anger is fueled not only by John's lack of responsiveness to her but by childhood humiliations at the hands of her father and her brothers.

The driving motivation for destructive communications usually has two more or less distinct roots, one in childhood and one in the ongoing adult conflict. Chronic, destructive styles of reacting to other people usually have persisted from an early age. Typically these styles of talking and relating have created a vicious circle. For example, a child learns to handle his loneliness by acting indifferently to people. Later in life his remote style discourages loved ones from getting close to him. This reconfirms for him the necessity of remaining isolated. As another example, a man learns from his father to relate to women by intimidating them. When he becomes a husband, his demeaning attitudes toward his wife lead her to react angrily. He becomes convinced that "women need to be taught a lesson." A girl may learn that the best way to handle conflict is to fake compliance despite simmering inside. She may repeat this in adulthood, confusing and antagonizing her spouse or children, falsely convincing herself of the need to continue faking compliance.

People who seek help from me frequently remark at the outset that their earlier therapies failed to confront lifelong destructive ways of thinking, acting, and communicating. My emphasis on love helps throw negative behaviors into more obvious relief. The ideal of love provides a standard against which to measure each person's communications and conduct. Without love as a guiding principle, therapy and relationships in general are likely to flounder or fall short of their full potential.

The emphasis in earlier chapters on principled living becomes obviously important in the creation of more loving relationships. Couples or families who come for help usually lack a set of coherent, rational ideas about what they can or should expect from themselves and each other. They don't have an articulated concept of love, including how to express and to receive it. They don't know how to insist upon the courteous, respectful communication without which the development of vulnerability and love is impossible. They may have worked with prior therapists who compounded their confusion by failing to stop or even by encouraging hateful expressions. The same therapists may have looked cynically upon love as an ideal by which to measure the quality of relationships.

Earlier I defined love as joyful awareness with aspects of caring, reverence, and treasuring. The definition, while simplified, has proven helpful to people in couples and family therapy. Love is essentially happy or joyful, even ecstatic at times. Depending on the viewpoint of the participants, it bathes loving relationships with secular reverence or religious holiness. It allows us to set the goal of communication as the nurturing of respectful, loving relationships.

Romantic love is sexually passionate love. Romance uses sexual intimacy to create or amplify closeness and mutual fulfillment. Romantic love is not an illusion. It expresses the most profound reality of human life—our capacity to take extraordinary delight in each other, to be joyful in knowing or experiencing each other, to be devoted to each other through the good and the bad times. In loving relationships, passionate love can become a part of everyday life. Lovemaking can become part of a reverence for each other and for life. It can make us feel deeply grateful for the opportunity for such love.

A loving friendship or marriage can provide healing. In the beginning of most relationships, fear and helplessness threaten to overwhelm each participant. Close relationships bring out the best and the worst in us. If the individuals can create a healing aura for themselves, intimate relationships can help to ameliorate the lifelong suffering that each person typically carries into the relationship.

Love is not the same as a relationship. Love can be felt by a person without any reciprocity or mutuality with the other person. We can love people who have disappeared from our lives, and people we've never met in the flesh. Similarly, we also love persons who don't love us, who have rejected us, or who have betrayed us. Love is our feeling toward someone or something else. Unconditional love is possible because love is generated, felt, and expressed from within ourselves and does not require reciprocity or even a relationship.

Yet unfulfilled love is also deeply painful. Rejection from loved ones can easily cause us to withdraw our love. The challenge of life is to remain loving in the face of the inevitable vulnerabilities that it creates.

Loving relationships—the sharing of love and the expression of love in our everyday lives—is one of life's most fulfilling experiences. But relationships can also endanger and undo love. A loving relationship is much more complex than love itself. It requires hard work to maintain love through the ups and downs of a relationship. A loving relationship requires the building of trust.

Often one of my clients will arrive in the office flush with feelings of love but equally awash in fear. Most of the emotional pain that seems associated with love is actually caused by the relationship, including the rejection, abandonment, and betrayal that so frequently afflict human efforts to relate to each other. A feeling of love can restimulate the pain of earlier betrayals, losses, and disappointments. By encouraging so much hope, love raises the specter of disappointment.

The painful emotions so often falsely ascribed to love can occur in relationships that are hateful. When people collapse emotionally after losing someone, it's not necessarily a sign of the strength of their love. It can signal the intensity of dependency, fear, resentment, and other negative emotions.

Unconditional love is a source of strength. If a person can maintain loving feelings despite the inevitable frustration and pain of relationships, spiritual survival and triumph are enhanced. Attempts to heal or to remain safe by denying feelings of love can mire people down in helplessness, self-pity, and depression.

Therapy, especially when dealing with relationships, needs an articulated concept of love that makes sense to all the participants.

Differences of opinion about love should be discussed. Attempts to work without a conscious, shared ideal about love will communicate a potentially disastrous value—that relationships can succeed and be improved in a spiritual void. This superficial viewpoint will compound the confusion and despair already felt by those seeking help with their relationships.

By the time couples or families seek help, they have usually lost sight of love. Often they no longer believe in it. They may be bitter, cynical, and skeptical about the very idea of love. They need help in turning that cynicism around. In Sheila's case, the frustration and suffering she experienced drove her to behave in an unloving, destructive fashion. John, meanwhile, used compulsive work to plow his frustrated hopes and ideals beneath the ground.

Remembering, recognizing, and recovering lost love is a central aspect of healing relationships. I encourage couples to recall and to talk about times when they took delight in each other. I may ask directly about moments in the past, however brief, when the mere thought or sight of each other made their hearts sing. Often they have forgotten or repressed the wonderful promise that blossomed early in their relationship and then withered with unresolved, escalating conflicts. If love has been present in the past, then it's cause for increased optimism in regard to healing the relationship.

It is difficult to help people love each other if, as the helping person, we don't respond with warmth and affection to them as individuals and to their positive feelings for each other. A therapist should not feel inhibited about showing delight as people recover their capacity to love each other. Here again we see the principle of empathic self-transformation at work. It's up to us as therapists, teachers, parents, or friends to find in ourselves the capacity to treasure the people we are trying to help and to delight in their experiences of love.

Communicating hope can be difficult when relationships have deteriorated to the point that the individuals are treating each other badly. The therapist must try to find an empathic connection to each of the participants. This sometimes requires overcoming our own internal blocks to seeing the possibility of love within the chaos and strife. It requires understanding the fear and helplessness that drives people to resist loving and being loved.

Relationships can generate very destructive feelings and it's important not to gloss over these in our emphasis on the ideal of love. By the time parents seek help about their children, for example, they may be secretly wishing for the death of their offspring. Husbands and wives in severe conflict may be harboring murderous feelings toward each other.

People are usually relieved to know that intimate relationships frequently generate feelings of violence. These feelings reflect on the depth to which people feel dependent and needy toward each other. The therapist, of course, must be comfortable with his or her own similar reactions to stress and conflict with loved ones.

As a therapist, I usually talk briefly but directly about the importance of love, offering my definition of love as joyful awareness with caring, reverence, and treasuring. But I discuss my ideals only to the limited extent that people feel it provides helpful direction. Of course, I'll respond to any questions as best as I can. For more detail, I may refer them to one of my books, such as *Beyond Conflict,* or to Erich Fromm's *The Art of Loving.* Now I'll have this book to suggest to them. In the session, I try to focus on each person's life to find examples of love to help each of them understand what it's about. Fortunately, John and Sheila shared so many ideals with me that I could address them very directly.

When I point out the wide variety of experiences that can inspire love, most people can find illustrative examples in their own lives. A careful search may disclose that the person loved an animal, a tree, or a place in childhood. Perhaps there was an aunt, a grandparent, or a baby-sitter whose very presence made them happy. Perhaps a hobby or a book still elicits joyful awareness. Perhaps a recreational activity or a work project continues to capture their full attention in a way that delights them. Most important in couples work, perhaps there was a time—hopefully there are still moments—when the participants felt love for each other.

When people have always felt cynical and hopeless about love, they usually have been exposed to rejection and abandonment by their own parents or caregivers. When they have not recovered from these experiences, even after years of treatment with other therapists, I frequently find that they remain mired down in loveless or even hateful interactions with one or both of their parents.

If the person being helped remains unable to grasp the idea of love, the therapist should carefully examine whether or not current relationships, especially with parents, are reinforcing their cynicism or disbelief about love.

We learn about being lovable and loving while growing up in our families. If we have been damaged in the process, then further exposure to unrepentant, unreformed, or hostile parents or siblings will perpetuate the injury. Destructive relationships in adulthood can reinforce those early experiences. On the other hand, we are less likely to remain in self-defeating adult relationships if our experiences with our original families taught us about being lovable and loving.

Even without very negative childhood experiences or harmful adult relationships, modern society and modern therapy tend to disparage love. This denigration of love is seen in the emphasis on being "independent" to the degree of denying our fundamental interdependence with each other. From birth to death, our lives are so interwoven with others that when we try to handle life on our own, we are literally tearing apart our own fabric. To help people learn to love each other and to love life itself, the therapist must love people and life.

As therapists or helpers, it is our obligation and duty to nurture our own loving attitude toward life—our desire to be fully immersed in life and to take joy in life, but to take it with eyes wide open, with awareness of the complexity and even tragedy inherent in loving and living.

If we cannot feel and communicate this enthusiasm for life, we will fall short of giving clients and patients what they deserve. The same is true in regard to teacher and student, to parent and child. It is true in all our relationships. Nothing is as "contagious" as a loving attitude toward life—unless it is a hateful one.

People throw up so many blocks to loving and to being loved, the subject could fill a book. Simply asking a person to talk a little about love often results in the immediate confession of immense frustration and confusion. In therapy, I try to identify the person's ideas about love and then to trace them back to their origins in past experiences. In couples work, I keep a watchful eye on how the participants communicate their feelings, always against the backdrop of my viewpoint that the goal is loving communication and an everyday life bathed in love.

Toward the aim of developing healing in each session, I discourage hateful and destructive communication. It's important for people to acknowledge how frustrated they have become with each other; but it's more important for them not to take it out on each other. Anger as an expression of pain can be helpful; anger as an intentional tool for causing injury is not.

Rather than enforcing an artificial, superficial sense of love, I encourage the flowering of love by clearing away the threats and communications that make vulnerability too dangerous to risk. I point out negative communications each time they occur and encourage everyone involved to think about more nurturing or at least neutral alternatives for getting across to each other. I try to show people that respectful communication is required before anyone will dare to express underlying feelings and needs. Only when people are determined to avoid purposely hurting each other, can they begin to show their more tender sides to each other.

More directly than individual therapy, couples therapy provides the opportunity for people to learn how to heal each other on their own. The aim is for the participants to learn to heal each other the way I am helping them to heal in the sessions. The therapy ultimately becomes a model for what they can do on their own in their daily lives together. Life is difficult; relationships are among the most difficult aspects of life. Couples need to know how to help each other heal. The starting point is learning how to create healing aura in the session and then in the home.

Many therapists work in a somewhat similar fashion to what I'm describing. One possible difference is my emphasis on values and ideals. When couples seek help from me, I want to help the individuals to nurture and to love each other. Most of what happens in the session is measured against that ideal. It provides an organized way to analyze and evaluate what's taking place, as well as a long-range goal toward which to strive.

Our lives, especially with those nearest and dearest to us, can be lived from the perspective of maximizing the love that we can experience and express with each other. Love can become the central principle of our intimate lives—the ideal that guides our thoughts, communications, and actions.

Helping People Who Seem Very Different from Us

11

Can cultural differences interfere with people helping each other? Are gaps in understanding inevitable between young and old, men and women, rich and poor, and members of different races, societies, and cultures? How can these differences actually contribute to the creation of healing aura?

Many years ago, during a period of intensifying conflict between Israel and its Arab neighbors, a military leader from one of the Islamic nations came to me for therapy. Because he didn't want his own government to know he was seeking psychiatric treatment, the relationship was entirely secret.

M.J. had located me from the yellow pages. My name does not sound Jewish and not everyone at first glance recognizes me as Jewish. So I wanted to inform him as soon as possible about my religious and ethnic identity, including my concerns about Israel's state of war with his nation. But the therapy session began with such rapidity and intensity that I couldn't find a natural break during which to inform M.J. about myself. When it was time to end the session, he was still talking avidly about his issues. Afterward, I was left feeling that I'd failed to provide him with "informed consent"—sufficient knowledge about me to make an informed choice about my being his therapist.

The same thing happened on the second and the third interviews. I kept getting ready to tell him about myself but it always seemed like an intrusion on our enthusiastic work together.

Finally in the middle of the fourth session, I abruptly interrupted. I explained to M.J. that I had something important to tell him. First, I apologized for not mentioning it earlier. Then I said, "Since you are a devout Moslem and a military leader of a nation that's at war with Israel, you have a right to know that I'm Jewish and that I have strong concerns about the safety of Israel." I acknowledged that both sides in the conflict had their viewpoints and that I felt no personal prejudice toward him. In fact, I affirmed, I liked him very much and felt very good about our work together. But I was concerned that he might not want to work with a Jewish psychiatrist.

M.J. thought for a moment and then asked me, "Do you go to temple?"

"No, I don't," I replied.

He grew very grave. "That's very bad," he said. "A man should take his religion seriously. It would be good for you."

M.J. then took a few minutes to tell me how much I might gain from being observant and devout. It wasn't a rote lecture; he was clearly concerned for me.

We continued to have a very successful therapy relationship, one that grew in mutual fondness and respect, and that helped M.J. overcome his worst problems. He remained disappointed, however, that he could never convince me to become observant in my own religion.

As it turned out, this Arab military officer and I had a lot in common. Perhaps, as my Meyers–Briggs personality profile suggests, and as my political reform work confirms, there's a big dose of field marshal in my makeup. M.J. and I shared both a toughness and a vulnerability that drew us together. We both put a high priority on self-discipline and self-understanding, especially in regard to our effectiveness in achieving our goals in the world.

If my father had emigrated to Israel as a boy instead of to America, perhaps I would have become an Israeli military officer. If I could have become an Israeli military officer, it doesn't take much imagination to realize that, with an Arab father, I might instead have become an Arab military officer. No wonder M.J. and

I got along so well. We were truly brothers under the skin—potential field marshals in the same army. Only the accidents of birth and immigration put us into such different roles in such different cultures.

In regard to M.J. and me, our religious and cultural differences made us even more aware of our similarities. Our obvious cultural contrasts highlighted our essential similarities, making it easier for us to create a healing aura based on our common humanity and our special shared qualities. That we communicated so well across cultural boundaries tightened our bond with each other. It seemed like something of a miracle to both of us.

I don't believe that what happened was really that unusual. It is common for people of different cultures to recognize something special in each other and even to feel like soul mates.

Yet great concern is often shown about the problem of cross-cultural differences. We have justifiably become cynical about one group helping another, especially if the group that offers the help is more powerful and advantageously positioned. Too often the offer of help smacks of paternalism or manipulation.

Well-intentioned members of psychiatric and psychological associations frequently call for seminars and workshops to increase the "outreach" capacity of white-male-dominated organizations to other groups. Members of "minority groups" often react cynically to these efforts.

I have a somewhat different take on the challenge of bridging the gap between individuals from different cultural groups. It seems to me that the capacity for empathy is universal. Further, I believe that all people are fundamentally more alike than different. If we recognize this commonality with people from other cultures, barriers tend to melt. Furthermore, the existence of cultural differences can convince us of the necessity of working hard to communicate. As my experience with M.J. confirmed, cultural differences can motivate us to reach out more carefully and considerately to the other human being.

Romances, including that of Romeo and Juliet, often dramatize love as it flowers between people from hostile families or cultures. Soldiers abroad can fall quickly in love with citizens of the occupied territory. People are probably as likely to find soul mates or treasured friends among members of a different race or culture as among their own.

Take any group of Native Americans, African Americans, and European Americans, mix them together, and they are likely to make numerous matches across seemingly insurmountable, conflict-ridden cultural boundaries. It takes ingrained social prejudice and legal prohibition to prevent this spiritual cross-fertilization from becoming more widespread.

Cultural differences can, of course, produce communication problems and misunderstandings. A magazine story on conducting international business recently observed that members of some Asian communities will not accept an invitation to dinner until it's been offered three times in succession. They feel offended if their potential host gives up asking after they have said "No thank you" one or two times. It's an illustration of when "No" may indeed mean "Yes."

That, of course, immediately reminds us of the problem between men and women in America where men too often won't take no for an answer. They even mistake "No" for "Yes" in matters of sexual consent. Much more rarely, women have confused the picture by feeling socially obliged to say "No" when they really want and plan to proceed as if they have said "Yes." Men and women in the same culture can thus have as much difficulty communicating with each other as they would with foreigners and perhaps even aliens from outer space. Hence the success of the book entitled *Men Are From Mars, Women Are From Venus*. Often the difficulties have more to do with imbalances of power than with any innate differences between the groups.

The fact is that communication problems are commonplace even among people from similar backgrounds and even if they seem to love each other. Most of us must work hard to maintain good communication with the people who are most important to us.

Whether we are talking to family members or strangers, to people from our own neighborhood or from around the world—communication and intimacy require an extraordinary willingness to be sensitive to each other and to share in a manner that is mutually acceptable. No matter how close we are to each other, we must always be attentive to the differences, gross and subtle, between ourselves and others.

Cultural differences can help us remain alert to the inevitable need for sensitivity in communicating. The contrasts can provide a constant reminder of our need to see beyond our own viewpoint, enhancing our capacity to be understanding and helpful.

When I give a workshop in Harlem or Watts, it's obvious that I'm required to make an especially respectful effort to understand and to communicate. When a small black child wanders from the audience and comes to the podium to visit with me, it doesn't take a genius to see the need for special sensitivity. But in reality, we all need this special sensitivity from each other.

Membership in the same group or culture can sometimes raise more serious difficulties in communication than membership in conflicting cultures. I remember listening to an African American professor lament his discomfort and anxieties when he found himself in an auditorium full of "black nationalists," mostly members of the Nation of Islam. He found them so "different" from himself that their common racial identity was of no help. Their shared skin color seemed to amplify their conflicting outlooks and especially their very different socioeconomic and political identities.

When a group feels oppressed, conflict within itself can sometimes be heightened. The intragroup hostility can become very damaging. This has happened at times, for example, in regard to self-hatred among Jews, blacks, or women.

Genuine spiritual liberation—including the freedom to choose one's own values and associates—often generates conflict with one's group of origin. When individual members of a disadvantaged group become successful, they can reject anything that identifies them with their past. Some blacks who have risen out of poverty may want to act as if the inner city does not exist. Some Jews who have integrated into Christian society may want to believe "It can't happen here."

For human beings to become intimate with each other, they must accept their mutual vulnerability and approach each other with mutual deference and sensitivity. This is true for all people, including those from the same neighborhood, and even the same family. We cannot assume that similarities in background will make for ease of communication. Nor can we assume that great disparities in background will necessarily set us apart.

A responsible, loving American and a responsible, loving Iranian will have more in common with each other than with hostile, domineering members of their own cultures. Similarly, terrorists from divergent cultures, even if they hate each other, may have more in common with each other than with most of their fellow citizens.

There's another reason why cultural differences are often a benefit. It's well-known in psychology that people commonly project their fears and hostility onto those who seem different from them—women onto men, men onto women, blacks onto whites, whites onto blacks. But there's a deeper truth: We make these fearful projections even more readily onto those who seem similar to us.

When we meet people with backgrounds similar to our own, they are likely to remind us of members of our own family. For example, if a young Jewish man from New York City meets an older Jewish man from the city for the first time, he is likely to be reminded, consciously or unconsciously, of one or another older male relative in his family. If the new person seems somewhat like his domineering big brother or father, he may react negatively to him. If this young man has endured bad experiences with many older members of his own family, he might find it easier to relate to an older mentor from a group that's quite different from his own.

Similarly, in couples therapy it is common for partners to project onto each other their experiences with their own mothers or fathers. The more the partner actually resembles Mom or Dad, the more painful the projection can get. The same is true in individual therapy. If a therapist happens to share some physical characteristics or traits with a patient's abusive parent, it can become a large obstacle to the creation of healing aura.

Freud called this phenomenon *transference*—the projection onto the therapist of childhood feelings toward one's own parents. More broadly, psychiatrist Harry Stack Sullivan called it *parataxic distortion*—the tendency to see new situations in terms of earlier ones. These transferences or distortions are likely to be the strongest in regard to people who seem most familiar to us. They will be most disturbing when dealing with people who seem most like our nuclear family.

Thus it's mistaken to assume that the greatest barriers to communication or intimacy take place in regard to people who seem strange or foreign to us. To the contrary, they can be greatest with people who seem most familiar.

Conversely, it can be easier to relate to people who are very different from us, because we bring along less baggage from earlier experiences in our own families and cultures. This is a major reason some people seek interracial relationships and marriages. In the technical language of therapy, these relationships are likely to be less encumbered by transference phenomena or parataxic distortions.

In *Beyond Conflict* I introduced the metaphor of the conflict tree. Cultural differences and conflicts represent the branches and leaves on the human tree rather than the trunk or roots. All people have complex and sometimes contradictory needs for love, esteem, autonomy, freedom, and identity. All seek both a measure of peace and a measure of excitement in their lives. All live more by values and ideals than by simple-minded reflexes or instincts. Therefore, a person in touch with his or her own basic needs will be able to recognize the needs of others, regardless of the differences between cultures or societies.

Cultural barriers can sometimes evaporate when we approach people with an assumption of shared basic needs or common humanity, sharpened by fascination with the inevitable differences. In reality, we should approach all people in this manner—with comfort in our common humanity and interest in our differences. It's a formula that is practically guaranteed to encourage successful relationships. It is one of the bases of healing presence.

These observations suggest that getting together in groups to resolve intergroup conflicts may not always be best. With women on one side and men on the other, or blacks in one group and whites in another, the illusion of difference is worsened. The conflict is amplified when the contrasting groups bolster their identities by rejecting each other's humanity. Meanwhile, many individuals in the seemingly opposed groups will have a great deal in common. Many will have more in common with a member of the "opposition" than with anyone in their own group.

If we want to build bridges across hostile boundaries, it's often best to start with individuals instead of groups. If our family is in conflict with our spouse's family, it's probably best to bring together one or two members of each family. If we want to do something about racial or ethnic conflict, we may accomplish more by reaching out to a few persons than to groups.

Recently I was giving a seminar in a nearly all-white town in the midwest. During lunch at a round table I happened to end up with African Americans on my left and white Americans on my right. Because blacks are in such a small minority in the community, the whites were not accustomed to much contact with them.

One of the whites unwittingly made a remark that I knew would sound offensive to the African Americans. He said that African Americans often seemed too "touchy" or "oversensitive" about potential racism in white people. I asked the African Americans at the table if they would mind if I, as a white man, spoke to my white colleague about it. Asking permission seemed appropriate because I didn't want to sound patronizing by "standing up for blacks."

For the next several minutes, I explained how black people in America endure racist slights, large and small, on a daily basis. I described how a distinguished gray-haired retired professor had recently been stopped by a white traffic cop who wanted to know "Where did you get that car?" The policeman refused to believe that a black man, however distinguished, owned his own luxury sedan. I told another anecdote about a black psychiatrist, dressed in a suit, who was waiting for his Mercedes to be delivered by the parking attendant. A white man tried to hand his own car keys to him. I told him about the discomfort black women often feel when white women in shopping lines stand away from them or when the cashier fails to give them the same eye contact or courtesy that's been given to the white patrons. I talked about African American mothers who are more afraid of white cops abusing their children than they are of other black youngsters perpetrating violence against them. I mentioned how black teenagers, when they come to visit my home, are frequently stopped and asked for identification by suspicious local police.

When I was done, the black man to my left, a minister, had tears in his eyes. He was gratified that a white man understood; he was sad that so few did. He was pleased that I'd spoken up but he was disappointed that I was being listened to because I was white. He doubted that the whites at the table would have given him the same attention.

Why should it be so difficult for whites to understand the situation of blacks? How many white people would want to be black in America today? Why should it be so hard for white people to understand the pain of being color-coded in your own country as a second-class, inferior, or dangerous person?

The differences really are skin deep. Recently a friend of mine, B.B., put me in touch with a new colleague who kept remarking with obvious affection and delight, "You and B.B. are so alike." He would eloquently describe the shared qualities that he saw in us. What's so remarkable about seeing such a similarity between me and B.B.? My friend B.B. is Barbara Becnel, an African American woman. She's even much younger than me.

There is of course grave conflict throughout the world between people of different economic classes, generations, genders, races, nationalities, and cultures. Every possible difference between people—from where they happen to live to how they happen to talk—becomes a potential source of murderous conflict. By no means do I wish to suggest that different groups of people have no reason to fear each other. Often one faction of humanity is attempting to dominate or exterminate another.

We must never deny the devastating effects of sexism and patriarchy, racism, ageism, pedism (prejudice against children), economic injustice, and other expressions of domination and exploitation. But while recognizing the injustice in life, we should not deny our shared humanity even with those who commit injustice. If, in our outrage, we deny our common human nature, even with our worst oppressor, we become further victimized. We are robbed of our awareness of the universality of the human soul—that on a very basic level we are all made of the same spiritual stuff.

Recently, when I was giving a talk in Canada, a young man in the audience stood up and fumed with rage at me. He declared, "You come from an elite class. You can't possibly understand someone who's poor like me. You're a hypocrite for talking the way you do."

He went on in this vein for some time, until a couple of other people in the audience tried to criticize him for mistreating me as their invited guest. I ended up defending the youngster's right to confront me.

In the midst of the young man's yelling at me, I could remember doing the same thing in audiences when I was his age. "Yes," I reminded myself, "That's the kind of angry young fellow I used to be." I would have taken on any authority whom I suspected of hypocrisy.

Later on, people came up to me to express sympathy over the verbal assault on me. Perhaps they felt embarrassed at the apparent mistreatment of a visitor to their country. One explained about the young man, "He had some nerve accusing you of elitism. He comes from one of the wealthiest families in his province. His parents are from a rich mining family, but he's completely rejected them."

The young man thought he was attacking an elitist from a different economic class from himself. More likely, he was unconsciously attacking someone much closer to home, perhaps his own father. He may also have been attacking himself, perhaps to suppress his own impulse to return to the privileges of his class. On the other hand, there may have been some truth in what he was saying about me. Maybe he was attacking me precisely because he saw something of himself in me. I'm sure that angry young man and I have a lot in common.

All of us, women and men, black and white, Jewish and Christian, have suffered in common from an inequality of the most painful kind that gives us a shared identity. We have all been children. For most of us the experience has been, at least at times, so anguished we cannot recall much of it. In a sense, we all have posttraumatic stress disorder from childhood.

Even if we had relatively good parents, the inherent disparity in power between adults and children, the built-in dependency of children on parents, and the stresses in being a parent—all combine to make childhood to some extent a painful experience. Each of us, having been children, should be able to draw on our own reservoirs of fear and helplessness to understand the dreadful effects of oppression.

There's yet another leveling experience that we all have in common. We all live in mammalian bodies, with all their defects and limitations, as well as their remarkable attributes. We are all subject to disease and to aging. We will all die, often from ailments that cut across every conceivable barrier between people, including gender. In speaking of venereal disease, Shakespeare pronounced with irony, "One touch of nature makes the whole world kin.[1]"

Yet it is very difficult to share intimacy across imbalances of power or authority. In conflict resolution, all parties must freely participate. Everyone must "leave their guns at the door." That is, the conflicted parties must surrender the use or the threat of force.

Domination makes intimacy impossible. As I've described in terms of the "perpetrator syndrome" in *Beyond Conflict*, neither the perpetrator nor the victim wants to grasp each other's common humanity. If we are going to communicate across age, gender, racial, cultural, or economic lines, we must do everything in our power to reject any vestiges of power, control, or authority to which we cling. We must reject attitudes of superiority or domination.

Similarly, if we feel like the injured party in the conflict, we must not adopt a role of helpless victim. We must not indulge in emotional helplessness. To become close to another human being, we must refuse to be either a perpetrator or a victim.

Perpetration and victimization, domination and submission, are common facts of life that impede relationships of understanding or intimacy. To the extent it is possible to give up domination and submission, and only to that extent, can we become fully human with each other.

In situations in which one person seeks help from another, there is built-in inequality. The therapist, teacher, minister, or parent is almost always likely to harbor some unconscious sense of superiority. The recipient of the help is also likely to harbor feelings of inferiority. It can be enlightening to acknowledge the existence of these inevitable disparities. It's never useful to make believe they don't exist.

The aim is to reduce the inequality as much as possible by accepting our common humanity and shared basic needs, and by avoiding the use of coercion of any kind. Only when people feel relatively equal to each other can they enter into a healing aura.

---

[1] From *Troilus and Cressida*, 3.3.171.

At this point, we can return full circle to the original premise of this book—that genuine help begins with transforming oneself. Even when we are trying to help other groups of people, our help should be primarily directed at transforming ourselves and our own group. That's where we will take the real risks in confronting racism, sexism, or pedism—among our own friends, neighbors, or professionals. That's also where we'll have the most impact. Those who feel abused or oppressed almost never resent "help" from an outsider when the outsider is taking on his or her own group! They appreciate the risk and sacrifice that inevitably result from speaking truth to one's own group.

The principle of empathic self-transformation remains key. Nothing helps another person or another group as much as our empathic self-awareness—our willingness to improve our own psychological and spiritual state in response to their humanity.

Once again, the distinction between self and other begins to blur. Love remains the one ethical principle that transforms conflicts of self-interest into shared or mutual interests. When we look into our own individual hearts or into our own community attitudes with the aim of enhancing our empathic response to others, we in turn reap the benefit of changing ourselves for the better.

We are all very much alike—and very different. Each of us brings with us a shared humanity, including many needs in common. All of us have different viewpoints on how to communicate and how to live life. Differences between people—such as those of gender, race, and culture—can and do set people apart. At the same time, they can also provide the most fertile ground for respectful and loving intimacy. The fate of all of us depends upon the fulfillment of this truth.

Empathy and the Reform Spirit

12

Is reform work driven by anger and hate rather than by love? Does taking care of ourselves make us indifferent to the plight of others? Does empathy for ourselves make us less motivated to fight for human rights?

In the early 1970s, only a few years after going into private practice, I accidentally discovered the start of an international effort to revive lobotomy and other forms of psychiatric brain surgery (psychosurgery). Up to 50,000 lobotomies had been done to mental patients, many of them involuntary state hospital inmates, in the first wave that petered out in the 1950s. I decided to take a public and professional stand to stop the resurgence of this violent "treatment." This became my introduction to what would become a lifetime of reform work in psychiatry.[1]

In my inexperience and naivete, I expected leaders of organized psychiatry to join my efforts to halt the psychiatric mutilation of the brains of human beings. Although the campaign would be

---

[1] The campaign against psychosurgery led to the formation of the Center for the Study of Psychiatry and Psychology in 1971. The story of the campaign, as well as more recent reform efforts, are described in Breggin, P., & Breggin, G. (1994). *The war against children.* New York: St. Martin's Press.

more successful than I could have hoped, I would be very disappointed with the response from my profession.

Even after I disclosed that experimental psychosurgery was being performed on little black children in a segregated institution in Mississippi, the heads of psychiatric organizations rallied to defend the treatment. These same people defended the operations after I publicized how they were being advocated by Harvard professors of psychiatry and neurosurgery as a potential weapon of control against African American urban "rioters" and their "leaders." The lack of any scientific validity to the devastating procedures did not dissuade official circles from approving them. The campaign was successful in stopping most of the psychosurgery projects. It completely discredited racist, politically motivated psychiatrists and surgeons who became much more circumspect in their pronouncements. All this success came despite resistance to my reforms from within organized psychiatry.

In the beginning, I felt all alone in a righteous cause that few others seemed to recognize or support. Unprepared for dealing with public and professional hostility or indifference, I often became frightened, frustrated, and angry.

One of those attacking me was Leo Alexander, a famous Boston psychiatrist, who began to libel and slander me. Alexander, who is now deceased, had ample reason to feel threatened by me. Not only was he a prolobotomist and a friend to surgeons who did the surgical mutilations, he had another darker secret.

As a military officer during World War II, Alexander had become the chief psychiatric and medical investigator for the army at the Nuremberg trials that sought to ferret out and punish perpetrators of crimes against humanity. Alexander publicly claimed to have written the Nuremberg Code that established protections for subjects of medical experimentation. This turned out to be utterly false.

As I documented in *The War Against Children*, and in earlier publications, Alexander had instead covered up the atrocities committed by psychiatrists in Nazi Germany by failing to recommend indictments against them. In addition to my campaign against psychosurgery, I had recently published a magazine article disclosing for the first time in the popular press the degree of German psychiatric involvement in helping to bring about the

Holocaust. Alexander must have felt like I was breathing down his moral and political neck.

Eventually Alexander's libel and slander of me became so egregious that I felt compelled to sue him. During the legal action, my attorney decided to send Alexander a "Christmas present." It was a subpoena aimed at tying up all of his personal assets—prohibiting him from any major financial transactions—until settlement of the case. It was, of course, calculated to make life difficult for him while protecting any money we might win.

Without my knowing it was coming, a copy of Alexander's subpoena was automatically sent to me at my home. Like the original sent to Alexander, it arrived on Christmas. As I opened it, I thought the subpoena was directed at me. When I realized it was merely a copy of what had been sent to Alexander, I felt enormous relief. It also made me realize how much more threatened Alexander must have felt on getting the real thing on Christmas.

As much as I detested Alexander's professional activities—promoting lobotomy, exonerating Nazi war criminals—I did not feel that I should purposely attempt to inflict punishment on him. I promised myself that I would never aim my reform efforts at inflicting pain or at punishing anyone, even when defending myself against assault. I would aim at stopping activities that seemed harmful, unjust, or even evil but I would not play the role of avenger. When Alexander offered to settle the case in 1974 and agreed to stop libeling and slandering me, I felt relief, but not personal triumph.

My political reform work again illustrates the principle of empathic self-transformation. My determination not to take pleasure in causing pain relieved me of self-defeating impulses. It has made me much more effective. Avoiding hatefulness has spared my body and soul and has enabled me within my limits to remain rational. I have been able to remain in the arena of psychiatric reform for decades when I might otherwise have burned out or quit in frustration.

People often ask me why I take such risks in confronting powerful interests associated with my profession. I cannot know for sure—no one fully knows himself or herself—but I know where it began. As I've described in the first chapter of *Toxic Psychiatry*, I was a Harvard College freshman in 1954 when I first set foot in a state mental hospital as a volunteer. I was appalled at how the inmates were forced to live amid squalor and violence. I was saddened by their isolation from each other and all other people, and dismayed at what the psychiatrists were doing to them in the name of treatment.

As I sat beside a young woman curled up alone on the hard concrete floor in the corner of a dungeonlike ward, I didn't think "This is a mental patient." I thought, "This could be me."

The heart of being helpful—the creation of healing presence and healing aura—draws heavily on empathy. If we feel empathic toward other human beings, we will feel motivated to respond in a positive, healing fashion to their individual suffering. Sometimes empathy will also motivate us to take action in the wider world to improve the overall human condition.

The cultivation of empathy is very different from narcissism, which is a crippling preoccupation with oneself. Empathy opens us up to ourselves and to others, to all sentient beings and life forms. Empathy is not self-indulgence; it is immersion in life.

Only through a *willingness* and *desire* to do so can we remain in touch with the pain and suffering around us, from our closest family members and friends to humanity itself. Only through this same commitment to awareness can we bask in the joys of others. Because this is so difficult, it requires work. It is another example of empathic self-transformation—making the effort required to stay in touch with our capacity for love.

By contrast, the unaware self demands to be left alone, to be protected from knowledge of evil, to avoid sharing the pain of others, to run from the problems of other people and from life itself. Inevitably, the unaware self remains remote from the joys of life as well as the tribulations.

Empathy seems built into our fabric as social creatures. As already noted, one infant's cry in a nursery can evoke a general howling among the others. This is contagion rather than a more sophisticated caring about others. But as soon as children are old enough to toddle, some will amble awkwardly across a room to soothe a crying comrade with an offer of a hug, a cookie, or a toy.

Empathic awareness too often peaks in the teenage years, then withers on the vine of adult identity with its demand for conformity in the name of realism and practicality. Making a living replaces being aware.

Especially in this day of instant media coverage, it's easy to feel overwhelmed by the volume of pain and suffering in the world. Following the tragic bombing of the government building in Oklahoma City, President Bill Clinton appeared on television to reassure America's children. Not only can empathy seem distracting, it can become an impediment to conventional success. It's tempting to conclude, "I can't stay preoccupied with what's happening to other people. I've got to survive, to earn a living, to see to my family's needs."

It requires cultivation and determination, commitment, for adults to keep empathy alive. It must be done against the odds. But when empathy survives into adulthood, it becomes a force for the reformation of ourselves and humanity.

Empathy insists that we remain aware of the consequences of our actions for other people and all life forms. It encourages us to feel responsible as human beings for the suffering of others, even when we have not directly harmed them in any way. It prohibits us from wantonly injuring anyone, even our supposed enemies.

Empathy makes us yearn for justice for all people. It opens our hearts to victims of violence, prejudice, and injustice. It softens us with sympathy, even for perpetrators of harm.

Empathy makes us equal opportunity lovers—able to love people from any group, even those groups our families and culture vilify. Empathy makes us aware of *everything* that's going on around us, not just the neat package of events that happens to support our comfort with ourselves, our smugness and self-conceits, and our cultural biases and hatreds.

Empathy transforms tunnel vision into a wide-screen awareness of life. It is our window to the soul of others—to the heart of life itself. Once that window opens, anything can fly in and out. We respond to people and to aspects of life that once seemed trivial or alien.

Sometimes, empathy turns us into crusaders on behalf of those who suffer, from animals to people to Mother Earth. We become activists. At other times, it warms our hearts to those within our own smaller personal circle.

It seems easy to be critical of people who love humanity but not their own families, or to be critical of people who love their own families but not humanity. I have frequently heard derision of people who devote their lives to animal rights rather than to human rights. Myself, I've come to appreciate anyone's devotion to any aspect of life. None of it is easy; all of it contributes.

Empathy is a way of being—a self-sustained awareness of ourselves and others, an inclusiveness that finds space within ourselves for others, an openness that accepts even the stranger as oneself. Empathy is a viewpoint on life that opens us to the joy and suffering of others—to their whole lives.

Empathy is a force; it can motivate us to take stands on behalf of all sentient beings—everyone and everything that thinks or feels. If more of us allowed ourselves a full measure of empathy, women would find themselves treated as equals, men and women would stop humiliating each other, child abuse would end, racism would vanish, and definitive steps would be taken to end hunger, poverty, and inadequate medical care. The planet we live on would become safer from exploitation.

Finding Ourselves Through Principled Living

13

Why do people seek help? Can emotional suffering be caused by our failure to achieve a meaningful life? What's the best way to go about finding ourselves?

A mere 50 feet away, large as life in my 30-power scope, an oystercatcher goes about his business. With his thick, straight, fluorescent reddish-orange beak and matching red eye as bright as a marble, he looks like a creation from a cartoonist's imagination. With coal-black shoulders and black-and-white underbelly, he's appropriately dressed for a formal dinner, not for mucking about after mussels. He's been pulling the tough black shellfish from where they tangle with the roots of the grass at the edge of the salt marsh. Using his incredible beak, he works the mussels loose and then splits them open for an early evening meal.

After he's eaten his fill, he takes a long-legged dip at the water's edge, spraying water over himself with a flapping of wings. Then he climbs back onto the edge of the grass and preens himself in the late day sun. Eventually the oystercatcher takes flight amid a flashing of black-and-white wings.

Does he reflect on how perfectly he has carried out his nature as an oystercatcher? Probably not. He doesn't have to try to be an oystercatcher. He *is* an oystercatcher.

With a big dose of heredity, and often with help from their parents, birds naturally learn to "do their thing." Even among them, however, there is a certain amount of learning from life about such critical matters as selecting mates, building nests, rearing young, and avoiding predators. But compared to us, their roles and identities are relatively predetermined. They don't struggle the way we do with confusion and anxiety in the process of "finding ourselves."

Popular psychology books and an array of well-attended conferences and retreats suggest that many of us consciously strive "to be ourselves." We work hard to find out who we are and then to fulfill our potential. When our children are born, we don't plan their lives for them; we nurture them while they unfold in their own precious directions. If we love them, we want them to be themselves.

A number of modern psychologists have made the concept of a real self central to their theories. As a group, they are often called humanistic or existential psychologists. They have developed concepts such as self-actualization, individuation, and self-fulfillment. To some extent, at least, these ideas are a modern luxury requiring both economic security and a relative degree of personal and political freedom. They seem to be the product of modern, post-Freudian psychological thinking.

Dreams, guided fantasies, shamanistic trips to find our totem animals in the under and the upper worlds, the exploration of past lives, encounter groups, body work, drumming together, varieties of artistic expression, and a multiplicity of other techniques are used to put people into better touch with their real selves.

These "experiential" approaches can be stimulating and even enlightening, but they often end up lacking substance. It's not that there's anything wrong with them. Rarely are they harmful. Sometimes they are inspiring. They seem, instead, to be missing some crucial ingredients. By themselves, they tend not to get anywhere. It's hard to base a life on them. We know that for many people this search for the "self" becomes futile. They never seem to find or to express their unique qualities.

For many other people, the search never even gets off the ground. Personal and economic survival seems to drain people of so much energy, they have little time to think about ideal ways of living.

Amid relative affluence and security in this country, people none-theless feel as if they must be preoccupied with "making it from day to day" and "putting it away for the future." If asked about their creative or spiritual goals in life, they are likely to dismiss the question or to draw a blank. After the initial burst of enthusiasm for self-actualization in the 1960s, we have entered a period in which "hard realities" dominate the lives of people as much or more than ever.

My work as a psychiatrist indicates that it's rare nowadays for a person to seek psychotherapy as a means to self-fulfillment. They may turn for this inspiration or guidance to various weekend workshops but seldom to psychotherapists, counselors, psycholo-gists, or psychiatrists for one-to-one therapy. People mostly seek help from mental health professionals because they are suffering. Often they have suffered for years—even for a lifetime—before they finally take the step. They don't come with the hope of reach-ing new heights of inspired living. They come to handle the pain as best they can.

Despite modern emphasis in humanistic psychology, few peo-ple actually end up making personal growth a centerpiece of their lives. Most find themselves living lives that have more or less evolved by a combination of seeming necessity, short-term choices, and happenstance. There's no plan aimed at spiritual perfection or even spiritual development.

Yet people do continue to yearn for a meaningful life, for ways of thinking, feeling, and acting that spring from inner principles and accord with moral and religious guidelines. They may not be pre-occupied with how to explore and fulfill a more real sense of self or identity, but they wish their lives had more satisfaction, more direction, more meaning. This yearning may reflect a breakdown of older, traditional community ties and beliefs. It may also repre-sent the relatively recent liberation of the human spirit to contem-plate its own future on earth.

To be helpful to another human being, we must be willing to look beneath the struggle to survive or to reduce emotional pain. Not very far beneath the surface, an enormous amount of human suffering has to do with the failure to find a meaningful way of life—to find fulfillment. Often there are glimmers of what that life might look like. Usually they are vague shadows that lurk, more menacing than inviting, in the background of our awareness.

Frustrated in their attempts to find a more meaningful and satisfying spiritual life, people easily turn to shortcuts (chapter 7). Taking drugs to subdue emotional suffering is one of the most advertised shortcuts. Another is the attempt to "find happiness." The direct pursuit of happiness leads, if anywhere, toward self-destruction. Happiness can be a fortunate result of right living and good fortune. It cannot be guaranteed, nor can it be a goal in itself.

Attempts to make happiness a goal lead to hedonistic excesses, to drugs, to a preoccupation with oneself. Oddly enough, while psychiatry never talks about "happiness," its use of drugs implies that medications can create a happier condition. Psychiatrists would reject this implication, claiming instead that they are treating mental illness. The patient, most of the time, comes for help for relief of unhappiness and suffering. The psychiatrist redefines it as the treatment of an illness.

If we cannot pursue happiness directly, how are we to pursue it? In a sense, not at all. The pursuit of happiness should rarely if ever guide our actions. It should never dominate our life plan.

What are we to pursue in life, if not happiness? Life is lived most effectively through principled living rather than through a direct striving for pleasure, self-satisfaction, joy, or happiness. The challenge is to select the best principles by which to live and to find the persistence and courage to use them as guidelines in our everyday lives.

Many of the fundamental principles of life are generally agreed upon. Most people believe in honesty and sincerity. Most people believe in fulfilling contracts and taking responsibility for friends and family. Along with many others, I believe in respect for individual liberty and in investing life with as much love as possible. Since love is joyful awareness, a loving life will maximize our happiness. Overall, courage is required if we are to live by any set of honest, honorable principles.

Happiness cannot be guaranteed. Liberty is often precarious in both our personal and our political lives. Love itself makes us vulnerable to loss and to pain. Love can motivate us to make sacrifices that compromise personal pleasure or enjoyment. Living by the principles of liberty and love can put us into situations that threaten our very existence, as in defending loved ones or in promoting reforms that gain the enmity of powerful people or institutions.

Empathy itself doesn't guarantee happiness. To the contrary, it can be difficult to be happy amid widespread suffering. We can strive, as I've suggested, to overcome induced suffering. Nonetheless, it will catch up with us from time to time, and we will feel unable to handle the pain that's all around us. It's also difficult to be happy if we ourselves are afflicted with painful or debilitating illness. Many circumstances, largely out of our control, determine our degree of happiness.

The cultivation of empathic self-transformation is a profound aspect of soul and a partial solution to our spiritual emptiness and lack of control over life. Empathic self-transformation is not a narcissistic "me first" approach to life. It focuses on how to be fully present for the benefit of others and ourselves. It requires self-understanding and self-expression, but not self-indulgence. It doesn't require that we become chameleons who turn the color of our immediate environment. We don't become candy machines of the soul, ready to pop out with whatever is asked of us. Empathic self-transformation requires that we find within ourselves our potential to understand and to care about other human beings and life itself. We remain fundamentally the same while tapping our resources more deeply.

Although empathic self-transformation calls for responsiveness to others, it is the opposite of codependency—a compulsive catering to the emotions of others. Empathic responsiveness requires a strong sense of self. Otherwise we feel controlled by the feelings of others and driven to react to them, even against our wishes or our will.

Happiness or the lack of it can be an important signal about our approach to life. If we feel happy much of the time, we're probably doing something right. If we feel unhappy much of the time, we should reevaluate our principles of living and how we are applying them. But if we are preoccupied with being happy, we are on a self-destructive course.

Consistent with the principles of empathic self-transformation, if we are unhappy much of the time, it's time to become more caring toward ourselves. Each of us, including you and me, is as much a member of the human community as anyone else and has the same right to attend to the satisfaction of our basic needs.

Each of us must reach our own understanding about our basic needs and our values. Every human being is unique; on that, we all seem to agree. Subjectively, most of us experience ourselves as unique. We doubt, for example, that anyone can completely understand us or see the world through our eyes. From experience, we know that no one else has the same way of thinking and feeling as we do.

Our faces reflect the uniqueness of our inner selves. No two faces are alike. Even in regard to identical twins, loved ones can usually tell them apart. Between identical twins, their identities and souls remain unmistakably different. They are separate, thinking, feeling beings—often with very different personalities and aspirations.

Many of us also feel that we have a unique potential, a special individuality crying out for expression. Often we feel it stirring within us, even though we can't identify what it is. Usually we experience this potential as something creative—something that will give our lives a special flavor or coloration and, perhaps, enable us to make a special contribution to the lives of others.

Ideas about the source of our unique potential vary across the spectrum of explanations from genetic endowment to karma and God's plan for us. Few of us think that it's simply a matter of making a choice. There is an element of "finding out about ourselves" or "discovering our mission" or even "finding our calling." This presents two seemingly contradictory ideas about self-fulfillment: one, that we are influenced by forces beyond ourselves; the other, that we work hard to maximize control over our lives.

The goal of self-fulfillment is confusing and misleading. We want to feel fulfilled, yet we can't get there directly. We should live by sound principles, but that won't guarantee survival, let alone happiness. We need to live as principled a life as we can but, like Job, we may find that fate or God intervenes to take it all away from us.

Amid the inevitable confusion and uncertainty, experience teaches that life cannot be lived any other way except through sound principles. Intuition, reason, and experience also teach that liberty and love should be prominent among them.

Liberty has to do with the rules that limit what we can do to others—with self-respect and respect for others, with maintaining boundaries, and with understanding that minds and souls should not be coerced, manipulated, or intruded upon in the name of being helpful. When we're trying to help another person, liberty reminds us, "Your self-respect, autonomy, and independence are more important than my desire to help you—even more important than my fears about your future well-being."

Liberty is the context; love is the content.

Love, remember, is joyful awareness, an active treasuring. It is interest and curiosity, a sense of wonder and awe, a wish to know more, to experience more, and to share. It inspires gentle caring. Love can be felt for a specific person, for children, for people in need, for art or nature, for values and ideals, or for God.

There is probably no direct way to get in touch with our inner selves or to seek out satisfaction and happiness. It's best to live by sound principles—such as honesty, courage, liberty, and love—and then to await what unfolds. When, inevitably, we go astray for a time, we must return, once again, to living by the principles we cherish. The formula isn't all that difficult to understand; applying it is the work of a lifetime.

Being helpful to others begins with communicating these principles of liberty and love in an environment of healing aura. The therapist expresses these principles by radiating them through his or her own healing presence.

"Who am I? What's my real nature or my true self? What's my potential as a person?" We find the answers to these questions along the way of life without focusing on them. As we live by sound principles, including liberty and love, we immerse ourselves in the process of discovering—and rediscovering—ourselves and our potential as human beings.

Empathy and Forgiveness for Grievous Misdeeds

14

Can and should we feel empathic toward perpetrators of harmful actions? Do criminals use childhood as an excuse? Do people invent childhood abuses?

I have been a medical consultant in legal cases of horrendous murder that seemed to place the perpetrator beyond the human pale. They have tested my capacity for empathy and helped me grow in understanding.

A 16-year-old boy, Danny, hit a ball through the window of a neighbor's house—a frail, elderly man who lived alone. When he came out to complain, Danny hit him with the bat, dragged him begging for mercy into his own backyard, and strangled him to death. He then hid the body by burying it in the man's own rose garden. It was not a story that invited an empathic response.

Danny came from an apparently "good family" with wealthy, professional parents living in an extraordinary lakeside home near Chicago. He wasted his time in school, he never had a job, and yet he had his own car and lavish spending money. The local press condemned him as the ultimate spoiled brat.

What circumstances could possibly shed any light on the underlying causes of such behavior? To start with, like many people who commit violence, Danny suffered from impaired mental capacities caused in part by early injuries to his brain. As an infant, he had rolled off a bed and been knocked unconscious, requiring emergency hospitalization. At the age of 2, he became comatose in a kitchen fire that almost asphyxiated him. At the age of 12, he'd been knocked unconscious playing ball. The emergency room noted that it took him a surprisingly long time to "regain his senses."

Along with hints of a potentially much higher intelligence, neuropsychological testing showed impairments typical of "mild" brain injury. So-called mild brain injury can leave the victim feeling frightened, ashamed, helpless, and at times confused. Danny walked around with enough intact perceptiveness to know that his mind wasn't working right.

Danny grew up subject to repeated beatings at the hands of an unemployed, alcoholic uncle who was frequently assigned the task of baby-sitting him. On one occasion at least, the uncle became so enraged at Danny, he started to strangle him in the manner in which Danny would later kill the old man.

At the age of 14, child welfare was alerted by the school to bruises on Danny's face and head. To protect the uncle, Danny's parents denied that anyone had assaulted Danny. The family faked a story about Danny being beaten by a group of unidentified boys. Meanwhile, nothing was done about the uncle, who continued to threaten and sometimes assault Danny.

Danny's parents were both professionals. Although they seemed to love Danny, they were unwilling or unable to make him a high enough priority in their lives. To give Danny what he needed in the way of love, discipline, and attention, they would have had to reorder their priorities in regard to work and income. Like millions of modern Americans they felt they had to hand Danny's care over to a substitute parent and then to mental health professionals.

Like most of his peers, Danny experimented with drugs. Eventually he found that he could steal his uncle's alcohol and his mother's sleeping pills without being discovered. Unable to resist the momentary relief he got from these drugs, he became addicted, depressed, and suicidal as he entered his 16th year.

After a serious suicide attempt in which he overdosed on his uncle's alcohol and his mother's sleeping pills, Danny was admitted to a psychiatric hospital. He was put on Ritalin and Prozac. The stimulating effects of these drugs further impaired his ability to control his impulses. When his insurance ran out after a few weeks, he was discharged from the hospital. In retrospect, it was obvious he'd been getting worse on the medications, displaying increasing irritability and anger. The stimulating drugs were producing, in his own judgment, exactly the opposite effect from the one he needed. On the day he was discharged, he expressed fear to the nurses that he "couldn't make it out there" and "couldn't control himself on his own."

The week Danny got home from the psychiatric hospital, his uncle called him a "nut case" and "a loony," and beat him again. Danny ran from the house, taking his bat with him. As if begging to get attention, he began hitting a hardball randomly against houses in the neighborhood. Probably, he wanted to be sent back to the hospital but was ashamed to ask. Finally, he sent the ball sailing through his neighbor's window.

When the elderly man came out of his house and called him a "brat" and a "nut," Danny shoved his baseball bat into the man's face, bruising his lip and mouth. Danny was shocked at what he'd done and started to apologize. With blood trickling from his mouth, the old man threatened to tell the boy's parents. Danny became terrified and—amid images of his uncle assaulting him—he began to strangle the old man.

Afterward, Danny ran home and confessed to his parents. They said he sounded like a child who'd been caught stealing candy from a store. In fact, they didn't believe him. They only checked on his story several hours later after he couldn't stop crying. The police found the grave with one foot sticking out of it.

For a while after he was imprisoned, Danny felt little concern about what he'd done. He was worried only about himself. Gradually the nature of his crime dawned on him. He went through a period of sorrow and remorse, and then became deeply religious. He told me that, while he could not forgive himself, he believed that God had forgiven him. He asked rhetorically, "If there's a God at all, He's got to be a forgiving God, doesn't he?"

In the interview with me, he said many things about himself that hurt his case, indicating that he was expressing his true observations and feelings. For example, he confessed that he could control himself better when locked up than when on the streets. In jail, he felt happier and more secure than he'd ever been. He gave me negative responses to each of my questions concerning whether or not he was mentally disturbed at the time of the assault. He did not try to make himself look "mentally ill" even though his attorney wished to make that a part of his defense.

From my viewpoint as a medical expert, many factors in Danny's world contributed to his violent assault. Among the most salient were his inadequate upbringing by parents who were preoccupied with their own activities, his abuse at the hands of his uncle, his parents' refusal to deal with the abuse, and negligent psychiatric care.

In addition to his human environment, Danny's brain injuries and the stimulating psychiatric drugs contributed to his loss of impulse control. It is remarkable how many violent acts are committed by people with mild to moderate degrees of brain injury, especially under the influence of drugs or alcohol.

Nothing inflames rage as much as childhood humiliations, especially when combined with a sense of inherent inferiority. Whether it's a middle-class woman who uses her tongue to torture her husband and children, or a young inner-city youth who uses a gun to kill other youths, the actions are almost always driven by unrelenting humiliation in childhood. The perpetrators of especially violent acts have typically undergone horrendous humiliations, often with physical and sexual abuse at the hands of larger children or adults. Often they were forced to bear witness helplessly to the abuse of a parent or sibling they loved. In Danny's case, his brain injury and stigmatizing psychiatric diagnoses, added to his feeling that he was inherently inferior to others.

Humiliating feelings of impotence and worthlessness fuel most incidents of extreme rage in adulthood. Once a person is brimming over with humiliation, as in Danny's case, overreactions can be triggered by relatively minor provocations. Being bumped on the street or being sassed by a child can lead to a murderous response.

There is a myth that perpetrators of crime and violence try to blame their actions on childhood abuses. The opposite is true. Most people who are preoccupied with violence and hate tend to ignore or to minimize what they endured as children. They usually exonerate the adults who severely injured them as children and instead blame innocent people in their adult life. That is what makes them dangerous to others, even to strangers whom they imagine to be threatening to them.

For Danny's own sake, it's very important that he take responsibility for what he did. He seems to be moving in that direction.

For us as adults, it's most important to understand as best we can what happened to him. Then it's up to us to take responsibility for ourselves and our society—to work toward improving the world in which so many Dannys are growing up without the capacity to cope or to control themselves, let alone to thrive.

People will differ on their standards for forgiving another person's serious misdeeds. Most would require acknowledgment of wrongdoing, followed by a determination to make amends and to reform oneself. Others would say that forgiveness ultimately rests with a higher power. Whether or not we are willing to make a formal offering of forgiveness to another human being, a forgiving attitude lies at the core of healing presence.

Conversely, we should never communicate to others that they are beyond forgiveness. It can only make them feel more alienated and potentially more hateful toward themselves and others. Being judgmental toward a person is, most of the time, going to interfere with our helping them.

In general, when we are insensitive toward someone else, it may reflect more on us than on the other person. A teenage girl was having difficulty breaking off from her boyfriend. The young man didn't beat her, although he did become overbearing and insensitive. More important, he rarely gave her the tenderness she craved. So she went to a trusted older friend, Naomi, and asked for advice. This is what she got from Naomi: "You're spoiled. Shape up and face life."

Confused, angered, and grief-stricken by this response from her mentor, the youngster poured out her heart to me. "Maybe Naomi is right. I am spoiled," she wept. "After all, he is hardly ever mean to me. He just doesn't give me everything I need."

I asked in reply, "Didn't you say that Naomi recently started a new relationship?"

"Yes, she did. She's going out with a married man."

"Well, that probably explains it," I said. "If she's settling for so little, no wonder she calls you 'spoiled' for wanting more."

When we become most judgmental toward other people, it's usually about something we're struggling over in ourselves. When getting judgmental toward someone else, it usually turns out to be a negative judgment we've already made of ourselves. Unforgiving of ourselves, we are unforgiving of the other person. Frustrating our own basic needs, it is hard to see others seek to fulfill theirs. Naomi, for example, was probably putting herself down, "You don't deserve more than a married man. Stop complaining."

In a myriad of smaller ways—with our silence, with our lack of warmth, with a raised eyebrow, with a seemingly deaf ear—we communicate our rejection of the other person's experience. Helping begins with learning to fully accept ourselves and hence the other person.

Accepting, understanding, and even forgiving other people depend on the depth of understanding of childhood suffering. So much of the violence and hatred that drive people is rooted in the abuses that they suffered as children. This does not mean that all abused children become destructive adults. It does mean that most destructive adults have horrendous childhood experiences. And those abused children who do grow up to lead ethical lives will nonetheless carry emotional scars.

Only within the last 20 years have professionals begun to appreciate the devastating effects of childhood abuse and suffering on later adult life. Therapists have grown increasingly aware of the importance of revisiting these experiences in order to surmount their negative impact.

When we are trying to help people change long-standing psychological difficulties, recalling relevant childhood experiences can be very liberating. There are many reasons for doing this, among them catharsis and self-understanding. In Mel's case (chapter 9), he gained relief from his rage by tracing his desire to shoot his friend all the way back to his helpless anguish as he watched his father abuse his mother.

There's another reason that talking about the past can become healing. It helps us grow in our empathy toward the person, and that is bound to be helpful.

As we grow in empathy through understanding the individual's childhood suffering and humiliation, eventually that person will grow in empathy toward himself as well. Once that happens, we have given that person the greatest gift one human can offer to another—the gift of love, concern, and forgiveness toward himself. From that empathy for himself, in a wondrous spread of good effects, will grow his love for others.

Despite the fact that therapists and other professional helpers have only recently begun to understand the importance of childhood abuse, there's already been a backlash against this insight. The backlash has come from two sources: biological psychiatry with its emphasis on genetic and biochemical causes of abnormal behavior, and the false memory syndrome movement which claims that children and adults fabricate their memories of childhood sexual abuse.

The false memory syndrome movement—aimed primarily at protecting parents against supposedly false accusations of abuse—has made therapists afraid to look for histories of sexual abuse among their clients and patients. Yet these inquiries are crucial to insight therapy and to personal growth in general.

Childhood sexual abuse is mistakenly viewed as an outmoded "Freudian" idea. Ironically, Freud was an egregious promoter of the concept of false memory syndrome. As Jeffrey Masson pointed out in his book, *The Assault on Truth,* Freud at first recognized that the women in his practice were suffering from childhood sexual abuse. When faced with professional ostracism, he changed his explanation. Instead, he began to claim that children lust after their parents and the children then cover this up by creating false memories of being abused. It required 20th century feminist social criticism—not psychiatry and psychotherapy—to bring about any significant awareness of childhood sexual abuse.

Is there any danger that some therapists will foster the creation of false memories of sexual exploitation? After more than 30 years in the field, I have seen very few instances. Patients do not typically luxuriate in blaming their parents. Instead, they tend to blame themselves and to resist examining any negative aspects of parental behavior.

By contrast, I have dealt with innumerable examples of sexual abuse of children. Any county or city department of child and family services can document the frequency with which children are sexually abused by the adults who are responsible for them. In Danny's case, his parents fended off inquiries from their county's child and family services, and Danny's biologically oriented psychiatrists never realized the importance of the abuse in his life.

While an unethical, misguided, or disturbed therapist may whip up memories of abuse that don't exist, it is rare. It is far more common for therapists to overlook the obvious abuse that their adult clients were subjected to as children. In child psychiatry, it is commonplace to make believe that children become severely emotionally disturbed in the absence of any problems in their environment.

Nonetheless, there remains the risk that some children will be manipulated into reporting false stories of abuse about their parents or caregivers. Small children are impressionable and easily confused. Unscrupulous parents or professionals can push them to describe events that never took place. Some parents, embroiled in custody disputes, have encouraged their children to repeat faked accusations of child abuse. Some mental health experts, acting on behalf of the prosecution in legal cases, seem to have done the same thing. Meanwhile, the vast majority of incidents of real abuse go unreported.

Within society as a whole, the abuse of children remains far more rampant than most people are willing to admit. Parents, therapists, and other adults are far more likely to overlook child sexual abuse than to exaggerate it. All forms of childhood abuse—verbal, emotional, physical, and sexual—continue to be denied or minimized by many health professionals, including highly trained, experienced psychotherapists.

The resurgence of biological psychiatry has reinforced the trend to deny the importance of childhood suffering. Biopsychiatry accepts as an axiom that innumerable children are born incorrigible and must be drugged into conformity with societal expectations. Biological psychiatry also assumes that parents do a uniformly good job and that children are at fault.

Little or no effort is put into ferreting out the environmental stressors that are impacting on the child. Often within minutes, the doctor—typically a psychiatrist or pediatrician—decides that the child has a "disorder" or "disease" comparable to a strep throat or a urinary tract infection. The diagnosis is made without giving serious attention to any potential problems in the child's family, school, or wider environment.

This biopsychiatric approach encourages the widespread diagnosis of children, including not only Attention-deficit Hyperactivity Disorder (ADHD), but Oppositional Defiant Disorder, Conduct Disorder, Major Depression, Anxiety Disorder, Obsessive–Compulsive Disorder, and a host of others. In a tragic reversal of the truth, the child's conflicts with adults are blamed on the youngster.

Out of ignorance or a lack of resources, many doctors, parents, teachers, and other authorities fail to address the personal and educational needs of the children in their care. Other adults perpetrate harm more directly against children through rejection, neglect, abandonment, and emotional, physical, and sexual abuse.

Psychiatrists too often claim that they can find no history of abuse to account for the reactions of the children they treat. Parents and innumerable other adults—such as other family members, babysitters, coaches, teachers, physicians, and ministers—are quickly exonerated of any potential responsibility while the child's presumably deformed human nature is blamed. However, there's no way to know how well a child is being treated within the confines of his or her home, let alone within the homes of relatives, and in innumerable other settings.

Danny's psychiatrists, for example, never even asked if there were a history of abuse. Neither Danny nor his parents volunteered it, and they might have lied about it if they were asked. They would surely have minimized it, as they initially tried to do with me.

Danny could have been tried as an adult with the possibility of a death sentence. Even when Danny's life depended in part on my discovery of extenuating circumstances surrounding his behavior, his parents did not want to admit the culpability of the uncle. Only when I produced the social service records, obtained by Danny's public defender, did the parents begin to tell the truth about how badly Danny's uncle had treated him.

Danny's psychiatrists prided themselves in being medical doctors practicing psychiatry as a medical specialty. Yet they utterly failed to respond to real medical problems, such as the implications of his brain injuries earlier in life or the disabling nature of his addictions. Ironically, they were so eager to justify their pseudomedical psychiatric diagnoses, they missed the real ones.

Although a psychologist had found evidence for brain dysfunction, Danny's psychiatrists did not bother with any follow-up evaluation. They also paid no attention to how the psychiatric drugs were worsening Danny's condition in the hospital. They could see nothing other than a boy with a diagnosable mental disorder suitable for treatment with drugs. They felt no empathy for him. This kind of psychiatric mistreatment frequently contributes to emotional breakdowns and sometimes to acts of violence.

As I finish this chapter, there has been yet another television documentary promoting genetic and biological causes for violence in children. This one purported to be thorough and scientific in its approach. It flashed a few skeptics, including me, on the screen. But its thrust was straightforward: science is making progress in identifying and medicating children who are "born bad." The last segment of the program highlighted a youngster from a presumably perfect family who inexplicably became violent starting at age two. He was supposedly treated successfully with three different psychiatric drugs at once during his adolescence.

Our failure to empathize with violent children is not the biggest problem we face as a society. Far more important is our failure to empathize with *most* of our children. Rather than understanding and meeting their basic needs, we are now psychiatrically diagnosing millions of our young people and treating them with brain-disabling drugs. In the next chapter, we turn to the broader issue of empathizing with all children.

Empathy for Children and Childhood   15

Why is the exploration of childhood such an important technique for personal growth and therapy? Why is empathy for ourselves as children so important?

Understanding childhood is one of the most important aspects of self-understanding and therapy. Yet adults often find it difficult to accept this. Understandably, they resist the painful process of revisiting or exploring their early years of life. To make it easier to understand the significance of understanding childhood, let's begin with a child.

One year ago, at the age of 12, Seth was almost thrown out of the seventh grade. The school psychologist had diagnosed him as ADHD—Attention-deficit/Hyperactivity Disorder. He recommended that Seth obtain a psychiatric or pediatric consultation for possible medication.

The school had no legal power to force Seth's parents to take him to a doctor for drugs. Instead, they made clear that unless his behavior were more controlled, they would recommend his transfer to a school for emotionally disturbed children. They also hinted that they would delay that decision if Seth were started on Ritalin. They said that many children in the school were remarkably better adjusted as a result of Ritalin.

Instead of acquiescing as many others would have done, Seth's parents brought him to me to fight the school's pressure on them. They were ready to hire me as a medical consultant in a legal case against the school, but I explained that it would be less expensive and more helpful to gain the school's cooperation. I offered to attend a school meeting to reassure the staff that Seth could benefit through therapy without drugs, and to exchange ideas with them about how to help him.

My appearance at school was in itself astonishing to the staff. Rarely had a psychiatrist taken that kind of interest in one of their students. During the meeting, the teachers stressed that Seth was failing English and social studies, and that his behavior in those classes was the most disruptive. His psychological tests also showed "attention problems," especially in verbal areas such as word recognition and retention. He would memorize a word and than forget it the moment he tried to memorize the next one. Meanwhile, especially in English, Seth would talk out of turn and giggle with neighboring students, sometimes distracting other students.

Seth's achievement scores were sky-high in math and science, but about average in English and social studies.

"He's got the reverse of my profile," I told the assembled school representatives. "Mine were out the ceiling in English and social studies. I think that happens: When you're really good in one thing, sometimes you're not so good in another. But when you're a kid, you feel imperfect if you're not good at everything. When you're 'bad' at something, you think there's something wrong with you. To me, it looks like he's a future scientist or computer genius. The last computer consultant that came to my office could hardly string two sentences together. But today's computer nerds are tomorrow's millionaires."

The teachers laughed. All of a sudden Seth had become a person to them—maybe someday a successful one.

Seth did feel abnormal because English and social studies were so hard for him in comparison with science and math. Similarly, the teachers were less forgiving of his weaker subjects because he was so good in some others. They wanted him to fulfill "all of his potential." Altogether, it made Seth feel so stressed about English and social studies that he could not stand to think about the subjects.

Talking about taking his achievement tests, Seth told me he "freaked out." Instead of admitting it, he explained, "I acted to the psychologist like I couldn't care less." To cover up his feelings of inferiority in English and social science classes, he became clownish, refused to pay attention, and wouldn't take homework seriously. I was able to point out these connections in the meeting and the teachers were able to understand them.

I didn't tell the teachers about Seth's family in any detail. That was confidential. I did reassure them, "Mom and Dad have said they'll work on their issues, too. As in any family, there are conflicts that are probably adding to Seth's anxieties."

When the meeting was almost over, the science teacher said, "I agree that Seth really needs to appreciate how special he is. I could work out an individual science project just for him—one that will be all his own. He could work on it during the study hall I supervise."

The suggestion was greeted with skepticism by the other teachers and the principal. Why give more work to a kid who is already flunking two subjects? They wanted to give him less work and to make sure he got it done. But with my encouragement, they went along with the science teacher's wonderful idea.

One year later, on his first anniversary session in my office, I celebrated with Seth and his mother and father. It was a happy moment. Seth was glowing. He had brought his weakest subject, English, up to a C. He already had a B in social studies. He was getting A's in math and science. Except for a little too much joking around in English—where he still got anxious sometimes—there were no negative comments on his behavior. Overall, the school was delighted with him. In fact, Seth had brought credit to the school by winning a countywide award for his special science project.

Seth's parents were much happier now with themselves as parents and with Seth. His dad, who never had much sympathy or appreciation for "computer nerds," found a new appreciation for his son. At my suggestion, Seth had taught his father to get on-line. Seth had become his father's computer consultant! Meanwhile, mom and dad were learning not to fight over Seth within his hearing, something that had made him feel he was ruining their marriage.

Seth's parents also learned to back off from criticizing him about anything. Yes, anything. Seth was so sensitive that he knew well in advance when he was going to get criticized. He was a master at criticizing himself in advance. By the time someone else had stated the criticism, Seth had already been through it in his head a million times!

Let the teachers criticize Seth when needed. Let me, his therapist, bring up criticisms on occasion. I sometimes instructed him not to speak disrespectfully to his parents when he could instead directly voice his dissatisfactions and desires. Of course, my "instruction" worked only because his parents were now listening to his feelings. My "magic wand" helped with that. In session, he could point the wand at his parents, and they had to pay attention to whatever he was saying, even if they didn't ultimately agree with him.

Meanwhile, there was more than enough criticism to go around. Seth needed one place where he felt loved for himself, and now he was getting it at home. Instead of being critical, mom and dad were learning about unconditional love—the joy of appreciating your children with all your heart and being grateful for their existence in the family.

After Seth's anniversary session, when taking the walk, I felt sad thinking about all the other millions of children getting psychiatrically diagnosed and put on drugs. It makes these children feel that there is something terribly wrong with them. Sometimes they are told that their brains have built-in biological and genetic defects. What a thing to tell children—that they're biological freaks—when it isn't even true. Instead of getting more understanding and more individualized attention from their parents and teachers, they get stigmatized and drugged.

I worked with Seth alone on occasion about how his family's conflicts affected him. Mostly, however, I dealt with these issues as family discussions. On a few occasions, I met alone with his parents to talk about how their own upbringing had made them more perfectionistic, controlling, and judgmental than they needed or wanted to be with Seth. Neither parent had experienced unconditional love while growing up. I encouraged them to give each other—and their son—the love they had missed as children. It was all part of helping Seth, who needed help for his parents and teachers more than he needed therapy for himself.

Suppose Seth had received drugs instead of family therapy? Or suppose he and his family had received no help at all? By the time Seth had grown up, he would have probably been in serious difficulty. He would have been suffering emotionally from severe depression or he might have gotten into trouble with authorities. He might have dropped out of school and become, in his own eyes, a complete failure. His potential would have been unfulfilled.

Suppose that Seth, as a troubled adult, now sought help from me for the first time. As an adult, Seth would probably recall few of the details of his childhood. Like many new patients, he would probably deny the importance of childhood and initially refuse to revisit it in therapy. Helping him as an adult would have become much more difficult than as a child.

With Seth as an adult patient, my goal would be to help him take a more empathic attitude toward himself both as an adult and, in retrospect, as a child. Instead of giving him the care I gave him when he was a child, I would be giving it to him as an adult in the process of helping him to explore his childhood. I would take a sympathetic, loving attitude toward what he went through as a child.

Understanding childhood cannot be an "objective" process on the part of the clients or the therapist. It must be caring—filled with understanding and empathy for the individual's suffering as a child. I tried to help Seth's parents become sympathetic to their own childhood experiences, opening them up to becoming sympathetic to each other and to Seth as well. As I mentioned, I would help Seth in the same way if he came to me as an adult.

It's worth stating this as a principle:

> Empathy provides the basis for the most important *technique* of psychotherapy with adults, the caring exploration and understanding of childhood.

When painful memories begin to return, some patients begin to feel hateful toward themselves as children. "I was such a jerk," "I never did anything right," "I was lazy," "I was a slut from age ten," "I made my parents hate me," "Some kids are just bad," or "My parent had to beat me."

During Seth's treatment at the age of 12, when I asked him about something painful that was going on in the family, his first reflex was to say, "Forget it, Dr. Breggin. It's just me. I do this stuff to myself." As an adult, Seth would have said these same things even more emphatically. It would probably have taken him a great deal of effort to begin recalling significant childhood stressors, such as his parents fighting about him or criticizing him.

At its best, psychotherapy explores and makes vivid the childhood origins of unrelenting adult suffering. It also discloses the childhood origins of the self-defeating values and principles that guide adult behavior. But it is no help to look back on our early years unless we approach our recollections with a nurturing attitude toward ourselves.

When we understand the suffering that drives our adult self-destructiveness, we can much more easily relinquish the emotional pain and change our adult behavior. We can more readily let reason and love guide our thinking and our conduct. A living, vital awareness of childhood can liberate us from emotional baggage, making it easier to learn more fulfilling emotional responses and more effective principles of living.

There are many other ways to look at the importance of understanding childhood. It's a truism that the failure to understand human history dooms us to repeat it. This is especially true of our personal history where we have much more control over outcomes than in the larger field of history.

If we don't know why we are the way we are, we are likely to remain that way, for better or worse. If we do not know how we got to be the way we are, we really do not know who we are!

If we cannot understand the pain and suffering of our childhood, and the mistaken lessons we gained from it, we are likely to compulsively repeat our childhood patterns of responding. Men and women repeat the same failures from relationship to relationship, marriage to marriage. They repeat their parents' mistakes with their own children, passing on problems from generation to generation. Throughout life, they react with the same feelings of guilt, shame, and anxiety regardless of the situations they are in. They have to get angry and always manage to find someone to be angry at. They anticipate rejection and, sure enough, it happens again. The ways in which we compulsively repeat our mistakes and our failures are infinite. Liberation from these patterns can be found through identifying them, tracing their origins in childhood, and then replacing them with more mature alternatives.

Revisiting our childhood can bring pent-up emotions out of the darkness of amnesia, allowing us to handle them in the light of adult reason. The rage and hurt that we felt, when reexperienced and understood, will have less control over us during our adult lives. We can say to ourselves, "I'm not really enraged at my own little son, I'm reacting as if he were my abusive big brother." We can remind ourselves, "I have a new family now. I don't have to withdraw from them like I did as a child."

The benefits of revisiting childhood can also come from recalling positive experiences. Perhaps there was someone who loved us as a child. Perhaps mom was very caring before she became chronically ill or before she was ground down by dad's unemployment and alcoholism. Perhaps grandpa taught us about love before he died unexpectedly, leaving us to suppress our memory of him. By reexperiencing the love we once knew, we can open ourselves to love once again as adults.

It bears reemphasizing that these explorations of childhood must be conducted from the viewpoint of a responsible adult. The goal must be to gain control over our adult behavior, not to excuse or to justify our current harmful attitudes and conduct. We revisit childhood to master it—to gain control over previously overwhelming experiences and to replace the lessons we learned in childhood with a more adult perspective.

Many therapists and clients understand the importance of exploring childhood, while missing the main point about it. The single most important aspect of going back into our childhood experiences is to develop a more empathic, caring, or loving attitude toward ourselves as children and adults. The most painful, destructive attitudes we have toward ourselves are usually traceable in an unbroken line back to childhood. At the time there was probably no one available to shed a more loving light on our suffering. Now, as adults, we can revisit those painful experiences with a respectful, loving attitude toward ourselves. The sources of self-hate can be cleansed at their roots.

If we try to evaluate our personal problems without the illumination of their childhood origins, we are likely to make a very negative judgment of ourselves. Why are we sometimes so selfish? Why do we withdraw so easily? Why do we get excessively impatient or angry? Why do we pick the wrong people to love? Why do we reject people who mean well and genuinely care about us? Why do we have all these negative feelings whirling about in our heads, not only about other people, but about ourselves? Why are we driven by feelings of fear and helplessness, shame and distrust, guilt and anxiety? Why do we turn to eating, to drinking, or to drugs to overcome our pain? Why can't we seem to be more reasonable and more loving? Why can't we just decide to change and do it?

While judging ourselves harshly, we will nonetheless fail to improve our actions. Judging ourselves so harshly, we are likely to become increasingly hard on others as well, ruining any hope for loving relationships.

Tragically, our initial lack of empathy for ourselves can inhibit us from exploring childhood. Time and time again, patients initially refuse to look into childhood because they resist feeling sympathetic toward themselves. When pressed about this resistance to recalling childhood events, a client will explain "I don't want to be soft on myself," "I don't want to make excuses," or "I don't want to blame my parents for my problems."

Childhood trauma and suffering does not provide us with an excuse for our problems. It explains the origins of our problems while in no way relieving us of the responsibility to understand and to improve ourselves. The point is not to blame the people in our past, but to use insight into our past to refocus on its good effects and to free ourselves from its harmful ones.

If we feel helpless about our suffering, it's a mistake to focus on painful emotional experiences from the past. We can become devastated all over again, reacting with induced suffering from our own memories of abuse. We should feel relatively comfortable, safe, and emotionally supported by a therapist or friend before attempting to deal with emotions from the past that seem unbearable. We need to feel "grown up enough" to maintain our adult perspective on the suffering we recall from childhood.

On occasion people are able, at least in part, to explore their past on their own. A variety of popular books can be helpful. But the process is so difficult and hazardous that the understanding of childhood required the advent of psychotherapy in the 20th century.

Biological psychiatry reflects our ultimate failure to empathize with children and their suffering. To diagnose and drug a child, we must reject sympathy and understanding for the situation of children in general and for the particular child who stands before us. That psychiatrists, parents, and teachers so readily turn to biological psychiatry indicates the extent to which as adults they feel no empathy toward their own childhood experiences and hence toward the children in their care.

Parents and teachers don't need psychiatrists and pediatricians to provide drugs. They need more help in meeting the basic needs of their children. The average parent nowadays gets more training in how to breathe during labor than in how to raise the child for the next 18 years. The average teacher gets more in-house training and encouragement in how to diagnose a child as having ADHD than in how to individualize the child's curriculum to the youngster's interests and needs.

The psychological therapies imposed on children are too often lacking in empathy for them. On a number of occasions I've been in discussions with professionals who emphasize that behavior modification in the home or classroom has been tried before turning to drugs. Behavior modification—the systematic use of rewards and punishments—is too insensitive an approach to work effectively with many animals, let alone most children. The theory, promoted by B.F. Skinner, was developed and demonstrated with caged animals, typically pigeons and rats.

As it turned out, Skinner's behavior modification theories were wholly inadequate in explaining the behavior even of these "lower animals" when they were free to live normally in their own environments. Both pigeons and rats have strong drives for freedom and exploration, and both use their cognitive abilities to observe their environments and to make choices among their many options during their daily activities in the wild. Only when the animals are deprived of their freedom and forced into rigid routines, can their behavior be predicted and controlled by the systematic administration of rewards and punishments.

Even if they cannot give voice to their feelings, children intuitively see through behavior modification. They know it's one more way of manipulating and controlling them without caring about them and without meeting their real needs. Spontaneously, they react as if it's an attempt to treat them like caged animals.

Unlike caged pigeons and rats, it is impossible to control children with rewards and punishments, even when they are "trapped" or deprived of their freedom in the family or school. Often they will rebel and even fight to the death, rather than submit. That's human nature.

Instead of rote rewards and punishments, children need discipline that can be rationally explained to them, so that they can eventually agree concerning its justification. They need unconditional love and more personally tailored attention to their basic needs at home and in school. When parents and professionals claim that "everything" was tried before drugs, they rarely mean improved educational approaches that will catch the child's interest. They almost never seem to mean getting to know the child in a more personal and loving fashion.

We live in a time when children in general are being neglected. Throughout the western world, and especially in the United States, children are receiving increasingly less sympathy and understanding from adults. Their needs for love, discipline, education, and even the bare necessities of life, such as food and health care, too often go unmet.

There are multiple causes for our current disastrous attitude toward our children (chapter 16). But there is only one way to reverse it. We need empathy for our children and attention to their basic needs. If we can recognize our children's suffering, if we can put ourselves into their life situations, we won't turn to psychiatric diagnoses and drugs. We will instead try to discover their unmet needs with the aim of fulfilling them to the very best of our ability.

As therapists, teachers, ministers, parents, or friends—as adults in any helping role—we will be effective to the degree that we can empathize with the individuals we are trying to help or to heal. Each person will present a new challenge to us. Often we will be sorely tested in our ability to care and to understand. We must remain alert for our own personal fears that block empathy and love. We must be ready to transform ourselves, to make ourselves able to treasure the persons we are helping. We must devote ourselves to creating a healing presence—the heart of being helpful.

In the next chapter we focus more closely on what may be the single most important key in the development of our healing presence: empathy for ourselves.

Importance of Empathy for Ourselves 16

Why do we need a sympathetic, understanding attitude toward ourselves as children? What is the role of anger in self-understanding and how does it differ from hatred? What is the importance of forgiveness toward ourselves and others?

Nearly every day, I receive calls from the electronic and print media about the rampant diagnosing and drugging of children. The media want an "alternative" view, but they are unprepared for my position: instead of diagnosing and drugging children, we should identify and meet their basic needs.

The media often responds with "What about the child who hides in the closet?" or "What about the child who is failing at school because he can't pay attention?" or "What about the child who refuses to go to school?" Eventually, the child who bites or even kills people will be raised as a specter to justify the rampant diagnosing and drugging of children.

I frequently try to remind these reporters, radio commentators, and TV producers about their own childhood. I asked one reporter, "Have you gone to parents' day at your child's elementary school?"

"Oh, yes, I went to my boy's school last month."

"Did you sit in your son's classroom?"

"Yes, they made us sit in our children's places."

"How did it feel? Were you comfortable?"

"After 5 minutes, I wanted to jump out of my seat. I couldn't stand it. Made me feel like a kid all over again."

"Just *remembering* what it was like made you squirm! Imagine how it must have felt when you were a kid, sitting in the same seat hour after hour, day after day."

"Oh, I hated school. It just wasn't for me."

"Well, it's worse in school nowadays," I reminded him. "The classes are bigger. The teachers don't feel respected. The competition for grades is tougher. There's a lot more homework. The atmosphere is much more tense and noisy. It's even physically dangerous. Illegal drugs are everywhere. And when the kid gets home, often there's no adult waiting for him."

"Well, I just hated school. I don't know why."

"Nowadays, you'd be diagnosed with ADHD or perhaps something worse, and given drugs."

At this point, there may be a moment of silence. I wish I could report that the silence will be followed by recognition: "You mean, these kids don't have diseases, they just hate school?"

Instead, I'm likely to be asked with dismay, "You can't mean that *none* of these kids have genuine diagnoses or illnesses?"

Sometimes I'll review some of the innumerable reasons that can lie behind one of the cardinal symptoms of ADHD—the child squirming in his seat in class. I'll explain, "The child could have worms. He could be hungry or tired, or both. He could have lead poisoning. Maybe he needs glasses and cannot see the blackboard. But the psychiatrist won't check out any of these real physical problems, because he's already made up a fake explanation, so-called ADHD. Or the child may be developmentally behind the other children and unable to keep up with the class. One child I worked with had an IQ of only 80 and was getting B's in school but the effort caused so much strain that the teachers were recommending drugs. Or the child might be a genius, and be bored stiff. I've never heard of a genius or genuinely creative person who wasn't frustrated and even tortured by school. Or the child might be suffering from conflicts at home. Maybe he's watching his parents divorce, or witnessing them fight over dad's secret drinking and mom's secret affair. Or perhaps the baby-sitter is sexually abusing him. Or perhaps like any child, just like you or me often were, he's bored to death with that particular teacher or feels bad vibes coming from her. Teachers sometimes resent their jobs. They may not be getting the educational support they need. Perhaps they are in dire need of a teaching assistant or a consultant. There may be too many upset children for the teacher to handle.

For those people who already suspect that diagnosing and drugging children is irrational and wrong, listening to me frequently confirms their feelings and opinions. Rarely, however, does any degree of eloquence succeed in turning around the people whose minds are already made up. It seems to be a matter of intuition—either you get it or you don't. The depth of the intuition, in my experience, depends on how honest and aware we are about our own childhood suffering.

Empathy allows us to conclude, "If I'd been as unfortunate as that child or adult, I might have reacted or behaved as badly." What enables us to identify in this manner with a child or with another adult? We must understand our own vulnerability. We must recognize how close we have come at times to losing control of ourselves and our lives—how much we ourselves have teetered "on the edge." It also helps to understand how our own suffering has generated dreadful feelings and irrational thoughts in us. In short, we must have a sympathetic understanding of ourselves in order to respond to others in a like manner.

Both the Hebrew and the Christian bibles have exhorted us to treat others as we would treat ourselves. The Golden Rule—"Do to others as you would have others do to you"—assumes that we already have a kind and loving attitude toward ourselves. The Golden Rule asks us to be as empathic toward others as we are toward ourselves.

We can make these observations into a psychological principle:

Empathy for ourselves is the basis of empathy for others.

If we cannot love, understand, and forgive ourselves, we cannot love, understand, and forgive others. This is true for us as therapists, teachers, ministers, parents, children, or friends. It is true whenever we provide a human service to others. If we do not bring a kind and knowing acceptance to ourselves, we cannot give that gift to others.

Conversely, when we reject the suffering of others, we tend to lock our own misery into place. If we deny someone else's essential humanity because of his or her misdeeds, then how can we, in the light of our own misdeeds, accept our own humanity?

There's a deeper aspect to this kind of self-understanding: knowledge and understanding of ourselves as children. So much of who we are as adults has to do with who we were as children. It's difficult to become caring and forgiving toward ourselves as adults without a firm basis in kindness and sympathy toward ourselves as children.

To fine-tune ourselves to the lives of other people, we must feel empathy for ourselves as children. Without dealing with the anguish we endured as children, we remain hampered in our capacity to reach out to others who continue to suffer from the emotional and spiritual ravages of their own childhoods.

These observations can also be stated as a principle:

> Empathy for ourselves as children lies at the heart of our capacity to feel empathy for ourselves as adults, and for other adults and children as well.

A judge in a state court was criticized for being too lenient in the sentence he gave out to a rapist. Then he came under fire again, this time for being too lenient with a child beater. The judge defended the child beater by explaining that the beatings he himself received in childhood had made him into a better person.

It seems unlikely that the assaults the judge endured as a child turned him into a good man or a wise judge. Instead, the physical assaults from his parents probably rendered him less able to hold other perpetrators responsible for their reactions. His adult judgment was impaired because he could not properly evaluate what his parents had done to him.

This particular judge was seemingly too lenient on abusers. Many other judges, of course, are thought to be too harsh. In my forensic experience, lawyers still refer to some of them as "hanging judges." I have found that the most judgmental people have shown the least sympathy for themselves. They don't want to be "soft" on themselves or on anyone else. They need more sympathy for themselves as children and as adults. As people become more in touch with their underlying pain, they are less likely to inflict it on others.

Most of us struggle with being judgmental toward at least some of the people we are trying to help. We react to them with anxiety, shame, or loathing. They seem to offend our values and our moral outlook. We are tempted to declare them outside the human pale.

If we do not become more aware of ourselves, we will make these judgmental responses based unconsciously on our background and on our childhood experiences. Empathy and understanding of ourselves as children can help us to overcome these judgmental reactions. By understanding our own vulnerabilities, we can become more forgiving of others.

Empathy for oneself is key for both the helper and the person being helped. In working with youngsters with severe problems, such as drug and alcohol addiction, their personal discovery of empathy for themselves is a turning point. When these "addicts" begin to try to live a sober life, they are at first stopped dead in their tracks by self-loathing. With their minds now unclouded by intoxicants, they feel appalled by how they have wrecked their own lives and tortured their friends and families.

Self-hate and self-loathing are not helpful to these young people. These reactions do not reflect remorse—a rational, ethical self-evaluation. They are driven by a paralyzing sense of worthlessness. These negative feelings cannot motivate them to improve their behavior. Instead, the self-hate, if unrelieved, will push these young people to seek relief once again through drugs and alcohol.

Recovery from disabling emotional distress requires that they learn to take a more sympathetic attitude toward themselves and their suffering. Eventually, with help from their Alcoholics Anonymous (AA) fellowship, therapy, family, or other resources they can become empathic toward themselves, and toward those whose lives they have disrupted.

I have on occasion been honored by an invitation to visit and witness the AA anniversary meetings of young people celebrating their sobriety. It is a miracle to see dozens of teenagers, so recently filled with hate for themselves and others, striving to give up resentment and to relate with love to each other and their families. Gentleness and forgiveness toward each other infuse their meetings and inspire their recovery. In the process of forgiving themselves, they forgive others.

Forgiveness, however, is not something that we can freely dispense without going through the painful process of understanding what was done to us. If we forgive people too easily, we may be covering up our inability to defend ourselves. If we too quickly forgive the adults who harmed us as children, we may be hiding from our anxiety and guilt over what really happened to us.

When we first begin to see the source of suffering in our own childhood, we are likely to feel angry and resentful. The anger flows from the process of recalling painful and sometimes abusive experiences. But in reality, the anger was always there.

When the childhood sources of anger remain unknown to the individual, the anger can fuel self-defeating attitudes and behaviors. Unrecognized anger can make us become passive in our resistance to people or stimulate us to flare up irrationally against innocent victims. It can show up as illness in our bodies, as exhaustion, or as difficulty focusing our attention.

Forgiveness is one of the goals of understanding, but it cannot be accomplished by leapfrogging over real abuses. We must know how we've been abused before we can offer genuine understanding or forgiveness.

Frequently people speak eloquently about forgiving their parents, even for the most destructive behavior. At the same time, they refuse to show any forgiveness toward themselves as children in the same family. Ironically, they forgive the grown-ups who hurt them while refusing to forgive themselves as tiny tots. As backward as the logic may seem, adults tend to believe that their parents, and not themselves as children, should be exonerated of all blame for what happened in their families. This ethical distortion can lead to the perpetuation of harsh attitudes toward their own children, creating generations of abusive child-rearing practices.

In the early stages of understanding our childhood experiences, anger is more beneficial than forgiveness. Anger can help us to feel more esteem for ourselves. It can encourage us to learn more about what was done to hurt us. It can motivate whatever actions may be necessary to protect ourselves in the future. When we express our anger, it informs people that they must treat us better.

After a time anger becomes self-defeating. Chronic anger leaves us stuck, compulsively preoccupied with whatever or whomever has hurt us. Some unfortunates remain dependent on their parents for a lifetime, stuck in the relationship by an unforgiving anger. They cannot let go of their anger, and so cannot let go of the people they are angry at.

People tend to leave anger behind as they liberate themselves from the crippling effects of their past experiences. They become focused on the present and on future growth rather than on past injuries. When patients ask me, "Will I ever get over resenting what happened?" I reply, "Yes, as you learn to overcome the effects of what happened to you." Patience and personal growth leave old resentments behind.

Eventually, when we realize what we have been through as children, we begin to understand or to imagine what our parents must have been through before we were even born. Without denying what was done to us, we can more genuinely forgive those who injured us. We are more likely to want to do this if our parents have admitted some of their mistakes and changed their ways.

Hatred, unlike anger, has no redeeming features. Hatred for even the most abusive people in our lives is not helpful to us. Hate is profoundly self-destructive and dangerous to others. Like Ahab chasing the hated white whale, Moby Dick, we are willing to risk dying as long as it eradicates our enemy as well.

Hatred is a signal that we feel injured beyond repair, usually by abuses we endured when very young. Hatred says more about our own impaired state than about the person we hate. Empathy and understanding for ourselves tend to soften hatred and ultimately to eliminate it.

While empathy for oneself as a child is key to personal growth and development, and to becoming more helpful to others, it is discouraged in our society. Despite the call in popular psychology to be responsive to our "inner child," the tendency is to deny the suffering of any child—the one inside us, the one we once were, or other children.

Instead of encouraging a caring, kind, or sympathetic approach
to children, our culture now accepts child blaming as scientifically
valid. Instead of taking an empathic attitude toward children, we
"objectify" them—viewing them as "broken brains."

There are many social and political forces that inflame this soci-
ety-wide rejection of children and their basic needs. The profit
motive, for example, drives the pharmaceutical industry to push
diagnoses and drugs. The profit motive also drives psychiatrists,
psychologists, and pediatricians to push diagnoses and drugs.
Even well-meaning, competent teachers can feel driven to suggest
drugs by their frustration with intolerable teaching situations, and
lack of school and community support for individualized education. Sometimes teachers lack the social and educational skills to
do their job and drugs are an easy way out.

The same lack of community support, the same sense of inadequacy, the same misunderstanding and ineptness cause parents to
seek drugs as an easy way to control their children and make
them conform to expectations. Economic pressure on the family, as
well as dysfunction within the family, are major contributors to
the general neglect of the needs of children. They encourage the
resort to quick-fix medications.

Children often feel compelled to deny their real needs to accommodate the adults around them. It is easier as a child to blame
oneself rather than holding the grown-ups responsible. To blame
parents or other authorities can be much too emotionally and even
physically dangerous. The child needs to believe that the adults in
his or her life can be trusted. The child needs their love and attention and so doesn't dare to alienate them by pointing the finger of
blame at them.

Day after day, experience teaches the child that it's easier and
safer to feel guilty than to get angry at adults. Even with the best
parents, a child—out of affection, respect, and dependency—is likely
to take the blame rather than generate conflict with parents. Lack of
empathy for oneself seems built into the conditions of childhood.

Some children are actively taught not to feel sympathy or empathy for themselves. They are systematically trained to endure suffering without flinching. They are indoctrinated that it is wrong to

"feel sorry for yourself." They are told, sometimes repeatedly, "You're too sensitive." They are criticized for any kind of "back talk."

In conclusion, helping people to forgive themselves is an important part of healing. To become understanding and forgiving toward others requires a similarly generous attitude toward ourselves as adults and as children.

To reach a forgiving attitude toward ourselves often requires work. It is another example of empathic self-transformation. When we find ourselves feeling judgmental or rejecting toward others, we probably need to do the work of finding a more empathic attitude toward ourselves.

By paying close attention to our own spiritual state, by making sure that we are sympathetic and forgiving toward ourselves as adults and children, we enable ourselves to give the same gift to others.

Grateful Healer 17

Why should we feel grateful for the opportunity to help others? What role does gratitude play in our own lives and in the lives of those we try to help?

Of all the gifts given to us, it seems to me that being able to help others is among the greatest. Of all the things that helping persons can feel about their activities, gratitude is among the most salient. As I like to tell students, "If you feel grateful for the opportunity to help people, you will surely help many of them." This is true for any kind of help but it is especially true when we are offering psychological or spiritual help. Few experiences in life are as fulfilling as contributing to the emotional well-being of clients, patients, loved ones, or friends.

Making a life's work of doing therapy is both an honor and a privilege, something to be truly grateful for. Being a psychotherapist is a sacred trust. To be well paid for it is an extraordinary bonus.

I am, of course, not alone in what I feel. Many people in helping roles feel grateful for their opportunity to help and many connect it to their spiritual values. They are grateful to be parents, health professionals, teachers, coaches, ministers, mentors, big brothers and sisters, and volunteers in many settings. Often friends feel honored and privileged to help each other as well.

Nothing in my training prepared me to feel this way. In fact, I entered private practice in 1968 reluctantly and fearfully, without fully appreciating the joys and gratifications it would provide. Soon after I got started, however, I began to appreciate the miracle of being a psychotherapist. With rare ups and downs, that appreciation has grown over the years.

The profession of psychotherapy is so recent in origin that if I had been born a few decades earlier, I would have been deprived of any such opportunity. I would not have been able to know so many different individuals in such an intimate and profound manner. I would not have had the opportunity to share so many thoughts and feelings about their personal lives and about the human experience. I would not have been allowed to explore the ins and outs, the nooks and crannies, of so many intimate biographies. I would not have been granted the opportunity to touch so many lives so often in such a caring and often loving manner. I would not, daily, have been able to help so many people live more rewarding lives. I would not have been able to contribute to the well-being and happiness of so many different people, including not only my patients, but the lives that my patients go on to touch with what they have learned in therapy. Overall, I would not have had the opportunity to do something so interesting, so worthwhile, and yet so remunerative, all at the same time.

Gratitude is not enough a part of our daily modern lives. When Europeans first encountered Native American cultures, they described their religion as one of gratitude. Native Americans express gratitude first and foremost to the Great Spirit for providing life and all the other good things in existence. They are grateful as well to all the lesser spirits who carry out the Great Spirit's intentions, for example, the Three Sisters, spirits of the beans, corn, and squash.

All the great religions express gratitude to God and many religious celebrations are meant to memorialize this spiritual attitude. Christians, for example, celebrate God's gift of His only son. Jews celebrate their covenant with God and their liberation from Egypt.

Being a parent is probably the ultimate model for human service—bringing a human life onto this planet and then doing one's best to provide it a good start. Were more parents grateful for this opportunity, more children would grow up glad to be alive and grateful to give life to others. Most of what I say about therapy in this book applies equally as much to parenting. As parents, everyday, we must find within ourselves the strength and devotion to maintain a healing presence and healing aura in our families.

It seems to me that gratitude is a key to the creation of healing presence and healing aura. If our patients or clients or our children sense our gratitude at being given the opportunity to help them, from that alone they are likely to undergo a measure of healing and growth. Our gratitude informs them about their own worth and about the worth of people in general. It communicates our genuine interest in their lives and teaches them about the value of all relationships. Letting them know that it's an honor and a privilege can help relieve them of the guilt and shame so often associated with needing or receiving help.

Unhappily, a number of my colleagues do not feel this gratitude for the work they are privileged to do. Especially among psychiatrists, their work seems too imbued with stress and conflict, and even resentment. Psychiatrists, for example, are known to have high rates of suicide and drug addiction. Psychiatrists, in my experience, find their work considerably more onerous than psychologists, social workers, counselors, family therapists, and other mental health professionals who also perform psychotherapy. The reasons for this lie in the psychiatrists' biological orientation and their role of social control.

Psychiatrists are physicians. This background and training encourage us to adopt a biological or medical approach to treating people. We naturally turn to physical interventions and to mental hospitals. In addition to prescription privileges, we have certain other medically determined rights and duties. We have the right to hospitalize patients, something that only a few psychologists share. We have the right to commit patients for involuntary treatment.

It seems to me that the medical orientation and the special privileges and duties that psychiatrists hold dear and try to monopolize, can become a great, unrecognized burden. Because I do not start my patients on drugs or prescribe electroshock and because I don't send patients into mental hospitals against their will, my work remains more joyful and fulfilling.

Prescribing medication for people is not an uplifting experience for the doctor or the patient. Drugs cannot elevate the human spirit. They cannot empower people. They cannot bring insight or understanding, or the capacity to live a better life. As I've described in depth in *Toxic Psychiatry* (1991), in *Talking Back to Prozac* (1994, with Ginger Breggin), and in *Brain-Disabling Treatments in Psychiatry* (1997), psychiatric medications can only distort the processes of the brain and hence the mind. They can only reduce the psychological, social, or spiritual acuity and awareness of the individual.

Medication can blunt the emotions, sedate anxiety, or artificially stimulate us. In doing so, it actually disables us. We trade a reduction in pain or an artificial lift for a reduction in our capacity to think and feel. It's understandable that some people seem willing to sacrifice brain function for the relief of unbearable pain. People frequently choose to do this with illegal drugs, such as narcotics, or with recreational drugs, such as alcohol, as well as with prescribed medications. But should physicians or other therapists encourage this inclination? Instead, we should help people make better use of their brains and minds. We should find ways to put them in touch with their feelings and their capacity to manage and guide their mental and spiritual lives.

When we offer drugs, we disempower the recipients. We tell them, in effect, "You can't make it by using your brain and mind. You need less of yourself. To get by in life, you need to be mentally impaired, you need to be less than you are." Again, this is hardly a joyful or inspiring approach. It is dismal for doctor and patient alike.

A psychiatrist is not likely to finish his day feeling grateful for the opportunity to practice the trade of biomedical control. To the extent that we empathize with people, we will hate to drug or shock their brains. To the degree that we wish to empower others, we will loathe these treatments.

On ethical, therapeutic, and scientific grounds, I am against trying to help people by impairing their brains with toxic agents. As it turns out, it's also better for me if I don't do it. Because I do not begin my patients on medications, I have the opportunity to work with them as fully sentient beings. Because I don't start them on drugs, I must utilize my full self as a helping, sentient being. I can't get lazy or rote in what I do in therapy or it immediately shows up in my working relationship with my patient. I can't cover up my lapses or mistakes by fogging the mind of the other person.

I am also against *involuntary* or coercive treatment on ethical, therapeutic, and scientific grounds. I believe it's wrong to lock up people "for their own good." It also doesn't help. After several hundred years of coercive psychiatry, there is not a single study to indicate that involuntary hospitalization helps patients. Instead of empowering people, forced treatment encourages helplessness and breeds resentment.

Because my patients know I won't lock them up, they are likely to feel more free to share their true feelings. If they are struggling with suicidal impulses, for example, they know I'll listen, work harder, and if necessary, see them extra times during the week. Rather than drug them or lock them up in a crisis, I'll provide additional sessions. I will do this free or for a reduced fee if they cannot afford the extra expenditure for the emergency help.

Because I don't give drugs or lock up people, I must constantly draw on my own psychological resources. As a result, the daily experience of doing therapy provides me constant growth and renewal. Through the creation of a caring environment with healing aura, therapy becomes a place of inspiration and rejuvenation for me as well as for my patients. If the therapy becomes conflict-ridden or filled with chronic stress for us, I know by my standards that something is amiss. Instead of reaching for the prescription pad, I go to work with my patient to create a better environment for both of us.

Gratitude on the part of the therapist helps to equalize the imbalance of power and authority inherent in therapy. Charismatic leaders want their followers to be grateful to them. Genuinely helpful people feel grateful for the opportunity to help. A therapist who feels grateful for the opportunity to help is likely to foster more equal relationships. The therapist's gratitude prevents him or her from feeling arrogant and helps the patient feel less inferior or submissive. Gratitude for the opportunity to help is at the heart of healing presence.

On occasion, any therapist will have difficulty maintaining a healing presence or creating healing aura with one or another patient. The personal "chemistry" doesn't seem to work. When this happens with many psychiatrists, they turn to another kind of chemistry—psychiatric drugs. Instead, I work harder to understand the blocks, inhibitions, or conflicts being generated between me and my patient. I assume that the problem has to do with both of us, and I remind myself of the importance of my own empathic self-transformation.

When therapists lose their capacity for healing presence, that particular therapy experience will be limited at best. If for any reason the patient does not seem to be benefitting from the therapy, it may be best to encourage a patient to seek an *additional* consultation from another professional.

Suggesting that a patient obtain an additional consultation should never be presented as a rejection. It should never constitute an abandonment. It should be explained as a reflection on the therapist's own limitations and the patient's right to seek the best possible care. Even if the patient has a long history of failing to benefit in therapy with numerous professionals, our inability to help the patient should not be blamed on his or her "mental illness." It is far more constructive, and often more honest, for the therapist to share or to shoulder the burden. Eventually the patient may meet a therapist with whom he or she can work effectively.

To avoid rejecting a patient, I hesitate to suggest an outright change in therapists. Instead, I point to possible additional alternatives, such as a consultation with another therapist or the concomitant use of approaches other than mine, such as group therapy or human relations workshops. If another professional can be more helpful than I can be, the patient can discover this in the natural process of seeking additional opinions. That way, the patient will not respond to leaving me as if it were a failure or a rejection. When a patient decides to make a transition to another therapist, I offer to remain available until the patient solidifies a relationship with a new professional (also see chapter 11).

A patient might need to work with several different professionals before settling on the right one. In some cases, a patient might want to continue in therapy with more than one therapist at a time, because each one offers something different and special.

If psychiatrists and psychotherapists more freely admitted their limitations, they would more thoroughly enjoy their work and feel more grateful about it. They would not push to maintain an ineffective, doomed therapy while their patient becomes more upset or disturbed. More open admission of their limitations would reduce the number of times they feel compelled to drug, shock, or hospitalize their patients.

Gratitude can provide a guidepost for living, as well as for conducting therapy. As much as possible, we should organize our lives around activities that we are grateful to perform. This can include those that seem divinely informed or that seem connected to our own nature, to our own needs, and to the needs of others. Especially, we should organize our lives around things that we love to do—around joyful awareness, reverence, and treasuring.

Among my professional activities, writing is probably my most treasured activity. It's the one that I return to most consciously for spiritual renewal. If I'm feeling emotionally depleted or out of sorts, writing is the professional activity that is most likely to rescue, redeem, or renew me.

Writing, to me, is like breathing or eating. I can't wait to do it. It's both a natural part of my life and a necessity for my spiritual survival. Long before I was published or made any money from writing, I devoted a substantial part of my time to it. I would write whether or not I could get published. Ironically, writing is so much a part of me that I often forget to feel grateful for it, much as I forget to feel grateful for breathing and eating.

My feeling about writing provides me a standard for evaluating how much my patients enjoy their own work. If they seem to enjoy something as much as I enjoy writing, I know it's probably a blessing for them.

Doing therapy comes second among the activities I most love. If I didn't need to make a living, I would probably continue to be a therapist, but with somewhat fewer hours. I'd probably fill in the extra time with writing. Perhaps I'd do more teaching, if I could find a way to make it as relevant to life as therapy can be.

Reform work, including public confrontations with my profession about the abuse of patients, is a distant third in terms of joy and gratitude. It feels good to stand up on principle and to have a beneficial impact on society. Unfortunately, it's also exhausting, frustrating, and daunting. Earlier in my career, my reform work cost me dearly in personal expenditures of time and money. It has exposed me to a variety of risks and humiliations. I am grateful that I have a "calling" that demands so much of me and provides considerable satisfaction. The feeling, however, is not joyful, the way I feel about writing and therapy. The wonderful friendships I have made through reform work provide the greatest satisfactions. I have an international "family" of people imbued with reform spirit.

My work as a medical expert in the courtroom pays much more per hour than anything else I do, but it's the activity I'm least grateful for. As most Americans know from watching TV, working with some lawyers can be a trial in itself. The legal profession too frequently attracts competitive and hostile people, and the justice system breeds further competition and hostility. The work pays well, the cases have merit, and the outcomes sometimes do a great deal of good. But it's the least joyful of all my professional activities.

My lack of gratitude for my medical–legal work probably reflects a lack of healing in my own life. I need to find a spiritually more comfortable and fulfilling approach to this aspect of my life.

It results in no great harm when I feel ambivalent about something in the public arena, such as appearing on television or testifying in depositions and trials. In contrast, it's potentially very harmful for a therapist to feel negative about doing psychotherapy. In therapy, every nuance of ambivalence or conflict will be reflected, if not in our faces, then in loss of healing presence. To the extent that they sense our ambivalence, our patients will end up feeling that they are burdensome. They will be reconfirmed in their negative attitudes toward themselves.

Helping people to overcome suffering and to improve their lives should be viewed as a sacred trust, a privilege, and an honor. This is how Native Americans and other indigenous peoples viewed their healing roles. Much as we should be grateful for life itself, we should feel gratitude for the gift of helping others in our professional lives, our friendships, and our families. That we do feel grateful for the opportunity to help will in itself encourage healing in those whose lives we touch.

Is Love Enough? **18**

Is love enough? Is it impractical, simplistic, Pollyannaish, and humanly unattainable? Is it unscientific? Can anyone become more loving?

This book places empathic love at the center of therapy and life. It defines love as joyful awareness—a treasuring of oneself, others, and life.

The term *empathic* is used for emphasis. Empathy is an essential element of love. Empathy recognizes that all of us are cut from the same spiritual cloth, that we are equally deserving of respect, love, and the opportunity to fulfill our basic needs.

When tempted to cast out others from the circle of humanity, empathy restrains us. Knowing or imagining what others have been through, we cannot be smug in the certainty that we would have done better. Instead, we will feel grateful for our relative advantages and good fortune. Especially, we will be grateful for the opportunity to help because it brings out the best in us as we help to bring out the best in others.

IS LOVE ENOUGH?

It takes more than love to be our best as family members, friends, therapists, teachers, doctors, lawyers, ministers, bosses, or employees. We need sound ethics and principles as well, but most of these will draw on empathy and love. We also need good fortune because circumstances can overwhelm or destroy any of us despite our best efforts. We also need skills, information, and the wisdom to use them. Yet once again, with a loving, welcoming attitude toward life, we will more easily gain our skills, add to our store of information, and find the wisdom to make use of our resources.

IS LOVE TOO SIMPLE OR SUPERFICIAL AN APPROACH TO THERAPY AND LIFE?

No, it's the most complex and deep. The concepts of healing presence and empathic self-transformation are not easy to understand. They are even harder to apply. To base one's work and life on love is a subtle and profound challenge. It has required half my lifetime to dare to find love at the center of my being, and another substantial piece of time to begin to grasp what it means. I expect to be learning about love on my deathbed.

IS LOVE TOO POLLYANNAISH?

To the contrary, to see life through empathic, loving eyes is to remain aware on a daily basis of the suffering that everywhere abounds—in ourselves, in those near and dear to us, in our communities, throughout the world.

IS LOVE TOO EASY A SOLUTION?

No, it is the most difficult of all. As a helping person, I frequently work hard to overcome my own impatience, frustration, and lack of empathy by renewing my capacity to love. All the other solutions, from psychiatric medications to outright violence, are much easier. That's why they're so popular.

IS LOVE ATTAINABLE AS A WAY OF LIFE?

It's always a matter of degree. Revered spiritual leaders usually remind us that it's a full-time task to sustain a loving attitude. It requires enormous energy and concentration to live a principled life and even more effort to remain as loving as we can be. None of us succeeds all the time.

IS LOVE CONSISTENT WITH SCIENCE?

Biological psychiatry, although claiming to be scientific, is too simplistic in reducing human suffering to isolated biochemical imbalances. This defies rationality and has no scientific basis. Biopsychiatry ignores the complex causes of personal conflict and suffering, including the effects of life experiences, confused or contradictory principles of living, failures to fulfill creativity and love, and thwarted ideals or spiritual aspirations.

All the things we do in life, including the activities we call science, are based on values and ideals. A therapy that tries to escape from ethical or spiritual content will lose its soul and its relevance to life.

Meanwhile, there is nothing to prevent us from basing a "science of psychology" on love. A surprising amount of scientific research has already focused on empathy and caring in life and psychotherapy.[1]

WHAT IS THE ROLE OF LOVE IN PROFESSIONAL RELATIONSHIPS, SUCH AS THERAPY OR TEACHING?

Without love, any and all relationships, including professional ones, lose their vitality and wither. Without love, relationships tend

---

[1] Carl Rogers published many research papers on empathy in therapy. I have reviewed more recent research in chapter 2 of *Beyond Conflict* (1992). I would also recommend Erich Fromm, *The Art of Loving* (1956), and Carl Rogers *On Becoming a Person* (1961) and *A Way of Being* (1995).

to become destructive. As I suggested earlier, "There is love—and then there is everything else." The bad stuff—including indifference, hate, and violence—is the everything else. Only through love are we likely to notice and to respond to each other's genuine needs.

Because of its great power, love must be handled with careful restraint whenever we are trying to help a vulnerable person. Love is communicated as our way of being through patience, caring, understanding, and empathy, rather than through coercive or intimidating declarations of love. We must always respect the other person's fears about caring and being cared about. In professional relationships, sexual encounters must be ruled out and the helping situation must be made very safe.

IS LOVE PRACTICAL AS A SOLUTION?

Love is practical in that it can be applied to everyday living. My own life demonstrates to me how a person can move from a nearly loveless existence to one that is, at times, brimming over with gratitude and joy. Love is also practical in the sense that it works. The moment a person increases his or her capacity to love, life improves. Love enables us to see and to understand human life with much greater clarity and to spread its good effects to other people.

IS LOVE TOO RADICAL A SOLUTION?

As a solution to human suffering, love is not original. It is radical in the sense that it cuts to the core of the nature of human existence. For thousands of years, philosophers and religious leaders have spoken of the need to elevate the human spirit through love. This book applies the principle of love to helping each other in both our daily lives and our professional work.

Love cannot substitute for professional knowledge, skill, and experience. It cannot substitute for wisdom. But love can generate healing presence—the most essential principle in being a helpful person. Together, people can create healing aura, a psychological and spiritual atmosphere that enables them to heal and to grow.

CAN ANYONE BECOME MORE LOVING?

Love is a universal, basic need. If we have survived childhood as social beings, the capacity for love has been integrated into our brains and minds. Love is the wellspring of our humanity. Even when we make believe it doesn't matter, we continue to want to give and to receive love throughout our lives. We might as well make love the center of our lives. It already is. It's only a matter of accepting who we are.

How far can we take love? How far can love take us? That's the challenge that awaits each of us.

There is a way to live a better life and to make the most of what we can give to others. There is a way to heal and to be healed, to grow and to help others grow, to make life into a shared spiritual adventure. Love is the heart of being helpful to ourselves and to others. It is practical and yet idealistic, simple and yet profound, grounded in our human nature and yet an inspiration to reach beyond ourselves.

Each of us will differ in our understanding of love. Each of us is likely to grow in understanding throughout our lives. We can know, along this road, that many others have been here before us, many are now on the road with us, and many will follow. When we participate in love, we participate in the whole of human life—past, present, and future—as fully as we can.

Index

A

Abuse
  in childhood
    effect on adult life, 140
    induced emotional pain and, 45
  sexual
    of child, 35
    effect on adult life, 140
    false reports of, 141–143
Academic credentials, for therapist, 69
Academic process, competitiveness of, 69
Acceptance
  of limits, 21–27
  of personal inadequacy, 21–27
Adequacy, communication of, 24–25
Age differences, therapy and, 109–120
Alcoholics Anonymous, 161–162
Alexander, Leo, 122–123
Anger; see also Rage
  comfort with, 74
  hatred, distinguished, 161–163
Anxiety, freedom from, 32
Anxiety disorder, diagnosis of, 143
Armoring of self, 51–59
The Art of Loving, 106
Artistic expression, and finding
  of self, 128
Attention-deficit/hyperactivity
  disorder, diagnosis of, 143, 145

Aura
  charisma, distinguished, 7–8
  derivation of term, 7
  healing presence, distinguished, 7–8
Authenticity, human need for, 32
Autobiography, psychology as, 31
Autonomy, human need for, 32
Awe, holding therapist in, 21

B

Basic needs, 5, 31–35, 37, 70, 72, 115,
  119, 132, 140, 144, 153–154, 157,
  164, 175
Battering, rationalization and, 4
Beliefs, importance to individual, 34
Betrayal, by friend, 83–94
Beyond Conflict, 59, 72, 106, 115, 119
Biochemical imbalances, pain as,
  61–64
Biopsychiatric treatment
  as control mechanism, 43
  diminishment of, 73
Biopsychiatric treatments, 43–45,
  61–64, 67, 142–143, 177
  as control mechanism, 43
  diminishment of, 73
  induced emotional suffering and,
  44–45
  reaction of brain to, 61–63
Body work, and finding of self, 128

181

Bonding
  in childhood, 77
  human need for, 34
Brain, reaction to drugs, 61–63
Brain damage, from electroshock, 44
Brain-Disabling Treatments in Psychiatry,
    62, 170
Brain surgery, psychiatric, 121–122

C

Care of self, by therapist, 36
Charisma, aura, distinguished, 7–8
Child
  abuse of, induced emotional pain
      and, 45
  attitude toward self as, 157–161
  empathy for, 49–50, 145–155
  humiliation of, rage and, 138
  sexual abuse, 35
Childhood
  abuse in, effect on adult life, 140
  bonding in, 77
  exploration of, 145–155
  humiliations, rage, 138
  trauma, restimulation of, 94
Cingulotomy, 4
Circle of concern, 57
Clarity of thinking, diminishment of,
    73
Clinton, President, Bill, 125
Codependency, defined, 131
Commitment, fear of, 83–94
Communication
  destructive, 95–102
  difficulties in, 97
Competitiveness, academic process, 69
Compulsions, control of, 21–23
Conduct disorder, diagnosis of, 143
Conflict, life without, 66
Connections, mental, unreal, as
    symptom of mental disorder, 76
Contagion, of pain, induced emotional
    suffering and, 44–45
Control, lack of, 21–23

Control mechanism
  drug regimen as, 43
  electroshock as, 44, 45
Couples therapy, 95–108
Crisis, emotional, extreme, 83–94
Culture
  effect of, 33
  heroes of, 34
  values of, 32

D

Dalmane, 61–63
Defense of self, 51–59
  as self-defeating, 52
Depression, 67, 68
  major, diagnosis of, 143
Destructive impulses, 35
Dexedrine, 61–63
Distortion, parataxic, 114
Divorce, decision regarding, 100
Dreams, and finding of self, 128
Drugs, psychiatric, *see* Biopsychiatric
    treatment
Drumming, and finding of self, 128

E

Economic level, therapy and, 109–120
Electroshock, 4
  brain damage from, 44
  as control mechanism, 44–45
Emergency medicine, 1–3
Emotional crisis, extreme, 83–94
Emotional helplessness
  induced emotional suffering,
      45–46
  physical helplessness, contrasted,
      71–72
Emotional pain, relief from, 33
Emotional paralysis, empathy and, 41
Emotional safety, human need for, 32
Emotions
  intense
    comfort with, 74

as indicators, 33–34
recognition of, empathy and, 48
Empathic self-transformation, 5–6, 16,
    49–50, 105, 120, 123–124, 131, 165,
    172, 176
Encounter groups, and finding of self,
    128
Energies, allocation of, 42
Equality, empathy and, 49
Esteem, human need for, 32, 33
Euthanasia, induced emotional
    pain, 45
Experts, surrender to, 3

F

Facial expression
    of pain, 48–49
    recognition of, gender and, 48–49
False memory syndrome, 141–143
False reports, of sexual abuse, 141–143
Family therapy, 95–108
Fantasies, guided, and finding of self,
    128
Fear of commitment, 83–94
Finding of self, 127–133
Forgiveness
    for grievous misdeeds, empathy
        and, 135–144
    importance of, 162–165
Freud, romantic love, 58
Friend, betrayal by, 83–94
Fromm, Erich, 106

G

Gender
    recognition of facial expression and,
        48–49
    therapy and, 109–120
Genuineness, human need for, 32
Gratitude, for opportunity to help
    others, 167–174
Great Spirit, in Native American
    culture, 168

Guided fantasies, and finding of self,
    128
Guilt, freedom from, 32

H

Happiness, principled living and,
    130–133
Hatred, anger, distinguished, 161–163
Healing presence, 5–12, 16, 37–38,
    43–47, 69–70, 75, 77, 82, 90–91,
    93–94, 155, 169, 171, 174, 176
Helping relationships, limits to, 35
Helpless behavior, 34
Helplessness
    emotional, induced emotional
        suffering and, 45–46
    empathy and, 49
    induced emotional suffering,
        42–43
    mastery, contrasted, 73
    self-determination, contrasted, 73
Heroes, of culture, 34
Heroic healer, role of, 3
Heroic treatment, concept of,
    in medicine, 2–5
Hierarchy, of needs, 34
Honesty, human need for, 32
Human condition, 29–30
Human nature, nuturing of, 29–38
Human needs, 29–38
Human suffering, empathy and,
    40–41
Humanistic psychology, 129
Humiliation, in childhood, rage and,
    138
Husband, need for wife, 97–99

I

Ideals, importance to individual, 34
Identity
    empathy and, 49
    human need for, 33
Impotence, empathy and, 41

Inadequacy
    acceptance of, 21–27
    respect for, 24–25
Independence, human need for, 32
Individuation, 31
Induced emotional suffering, 41–45
    empathy, distinguished, 42–45
Inferiority, sense of, rage and, 138
Injury, grievous, forgiveness for,
        empathy and, 135–144
Injustice, empathy and, 40–41
Insurance programs, coverage for,
        69
Intense emotions, as indicators,
        33–34
Intimacy, helping relationships in, 36
Intimidation, as communication style,
        102
Invulnerability, as mask, 52
Irrational fear, overcoming, 21–23

J

James, William, 58, 65
Justice, empathy and, 125

K

Klonopin, 61–63, 65

L

Liberty, principled living and,
        130–133
Limits
    acceptance of, 21–27
    to helping relationships, 35
    in relationship, 100
Lithium, 63
Lobotomy, 121–122
    induced emotional suffering and,
        44–45
Love
    defined, 16
    expressions of, within therapy, 36

as guiding impulse, 29–38
lost, recovering, 105
romantic, search for, 38

M

Major depression, diagnosis of, 143
Malignant empathy, see Induced
        emotional suffering
Mandela, Nelson, 72
Manipulation, 29–30
Mantra, development of, 94
Mastery
    empathy and, 49
    helplessness, contrasted, 73
Materialism, effect of, 64
Medications, psychiatric, see
        Biopsychiatric treatment
Men Are From Mars, Women Are From
        Venus, 112
Menace, mask of, 52
Mental connections, unreal, as
        symptom of mental disorder, 76
Monastic life, following, 38
Murder, commission of, empathy and,
        135–144
Mythologies, influence of, 64

N

Narcissism, romantic love, 58
Native American cultures, gratitude
        in, 168
Needs of therapist, 37

O

Obsessions, control of, 21–23
Obsessive-compulsive disorder, 143
Oppositional defiant disorder,
        diagnosis of, 143
Others, withdrawing from, induced
        emotional suffering, 42–43
Overwhelm state, induced emotional
        suffering, 42–43, 47

P

Pain
    contagion of, induced emotional
        suffering and, 44–45
    facial expression of, 48–49
    of others, overwhelming from, 47
    suppression of, avoiding, 33
Pain relief, giving, 33
Paralysis, emotional, empathy and,
    41
Parataxic distortion, 114
Past lives, and finding of self, 128
Paxil, 65
Pets, love of, 58–59
Pharmacology, psychiatric, *see*
    Biopsychiatric treatment
Physical helplessness
    emotional helplessness, contrasted,
        71–72
Political reform, 121–126
Powerlessness, empathy and, 49
Principled living, 127–133
Prozac, 61–63, 65, 67
Psychiatric drugs, *see* Biopsychiatric
    treatment
Psychology, as autobiography, 31
Psychopharmacology, 3
Psychosis, defined, 76
Psychosurgery, 121–122
Psychotherapy training institutes,
    establishment of, 69–70

R

Racial diversity, therapy and, 109–120
Rage
    childhood humiliation and, 138
    sense of inferiority and, 138
    toward therapist, 56
Rationalization, battery and, 4
Real self, finding of, 127–133
Recognition of emotions, empathy
    and, 48
Reform, political, 121–126

Relationship limits, 100
Relief from suffering, human need for,
    33
Religious experiences, harm from, 38
Restraint, as heroic treatment, 4
Role, of heroic healer, 3
Romantic love
    Freud, 58
    search for, 38

S

Safety, emotional, human need for, 32
Satisfaction, spiritual, human need for,
    38
Saving patient, extreme measures for, 2
Schizophrenia, 101
Security, human need for, 32
Self
    as child, empathy for, 145–155
    finding of, 127–133
Self-actualization, 31
Self-control, empathy and, 49
Self-determination, helplessness,
    contrasted, 73
Self-fulfillment, psychotherapy as
    means to, 129
Self-realization, 31
Sexual abuse, of child, 35
    effect on adult life, 140
    false reports of, 141–143
Shamanistic trips, and finding of self,
    128
Shame, freedom from, 32
Shock treatment, 64
Sincerity, human need for, 32
Skinner, B.F., 153
Social contacts, avoidance of, during
    therapy, 36
Space, defense of, 54–55
Specialists, in medicine, 3
Speech, destructive ways of, 96
Spiritual emergency, treating, 83–94
Spiritual satisfaction, human need for,
    38

Spiritual void, 66
Spouse, need for other, 97–99
Suffering
    relief from, human need for, 33
    responding to, 42
Sullivan, Harry Stack, 114
Suppression of pain, avoiding, 33
Surgery, on brain, psychiatric,
        psychosurgery, 121–122
Survival needs, 34

T

Talking, destructive ways of, 96
Talking Back to Prozac, 62, 170
Thinking, clarity of, diminishment,
        with biopsychiatric treatment, 73
Totem animals, and finding of self, 128
Toxic Psychiatry, 62, 123
Traditional sources of knowledge, loss
        of faith in, 64
Training institutes, in psychotherapy,
        establishment of, 69–70
Transference, 114
Trauma, childhood, restimulation of,
        94

V

Values
    cultural, 32
    importance to individual, 34
    sharing of, 97
The Varieties of Religious Experience, 65
Violence, commission of, empathy
        and, 135–144
Vulnerability, 51–59
    showing, 21–27

W

The War Against Children, 122
Will power, 21–23
Withdrawing from others, induced
        emotional suffering, 42–43

X

Xanax, 63, 65

Z

Zoloft, 65

Springer Publishing Company

Counseling Adults in Transition, 2nd Edition
Linking Practice with Theory

Nancy K. Schlossberg, EdD
Elinor B. Waters, EdD,
Jane Goodman, PhD

In this updated edition of a highly successful text, the authors expand on their transition model, which offers effective adult counseling through the integration of empirical knowledge and theory with practice. The authors com-

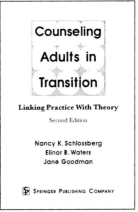

bine an understanding of adult development with practical strategies for counseling clients in personal and professional transition. A framework is provided for individual, group, and work settings. The final chapter goes beyond intervention to discuss issues such as consulting and advocacy.

Contents:

Contributions of Adult Development Theories to the Transition Framework • The Transition Framework • A Framework for Helping: Factors that Influence Negotiating the Transition • What Counselors Hear About Individual Transitions • What Counselors Hear About Relationship Transitions • What Counselors Hear About Work Transitions • What Can Counselors Do to Help Individuals in Transition? • What Can Counselors Do in Groups to Help Adults in Transition? • Group Counseling Practice

1995   320pp   0-8261-4231-1   hardcover

536 Broadway, New York, NY 10012-3955 • (212) 431-4370 • Fax (212) 941-7842

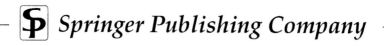

Springer Publishing Company

Brain-Disabling Treatments in Psychiatry

Drugs, Electroshock, and the Role of the FDA

Peter Breggin, MD

This book documents renowned psychiatrist Peter Breggin's vehement anti-drug stance in treating psychiatric disorders. The volume is intended to alert mental health professionals to the dangers of a professional preference for and an over use of drug interventions. Based in his own extensive clinical experience, Breggin carefully reviews dozens of commonly used psychiatric drugs and alerts the reader to their often disrupting side effects and dangers.

The volume illustrates the many inherent flaws of clinical trials and the FDA's drug approval process. The principles of this book are balanced by the alternative view that psychological, social, educational, and spiritual therapeutic approaches are successful in helping individuals to overcome their personal suffering.

Contents:

The Brain-Disabling Principle of Psychiatric Treatment • Deactivation Syndrome (Chemical Lobotomy) Caused by Neuroleptics • Neuroleptic-Induced Acute Anguish, Including Agitation, Despair and Depression • Neuroleptic Malignant Syndrome, Tardive Dyskinesia, Tardive Dystonia and Tardive Akathisia • Neuroleptic-Induced Brain Damage, Persistent Cognitive Deficits, Dementia, and Psychosis • Antidepressants, Including New Information of Prozac-Induced Violence and Suicide • Lithium and Other Drugs for Bipolar Disorder • Electroshock for Depression • Stimulants for Children, Including an Analysis of ADHD • Minor Tranquilizers Including New Information on Behavioral Abnormalities Caused by Xanax and Halcion • Drug Companies and the FDA: Failed Mandates

1997 320pp (est.) 0-8261-9490-7 hard

536 Broadway, New York, NY 10012-3955 • (212) 431-4370 • Fax (212) 941-7842

Springer Publishing Company

Logotherapy for the Helping Professional
Meaningful Social Work
David Guttmann, DSW

In this useful resource, the author explains the pioneering work of Dr. Viktor Frankl and his theories of logotherapy. This volume will enable helping professionals to supplement traditional methods of psychotherapy with logotherapy techniques in order to improve their effectiveness through clearer understanding of their clients' problems. Professionals can then derive greater personal meaning and satisfaction from their work, thereby lessening the potential for stress and burnout. This volume addresses therapists, clinical social workers, and counselors.

Contents:

I: Major Concepts in Logotherapy. The Development of Logotherapy • Logotherapy and Psychoanalysis: Similarities and Differences • The Noetic or Spiritual Dimension • The "Tragic Triad": Logotherapy's Attitude to Guilt, Suffering, and Death **II: Logotherapeutic Treatment and Application.** Paradoxical Intention as a Special Logotherapeutic Technique • "Dereflection" as Counteracting Behavior • Other Logotherapeutic Techniques • The "Socratic Dialogue" Logotherapy's Main Tool in Helping Seekers Search for Meaning **III. Research in the Service of Logotherapy.** Research on Major Logotherapeutic Concepts • Further Developments in Logotherapeutic Research

1995   320pp   0-8261-9020-0   hardcover

536 Broadway, New York, NY 10012-3955 • (212) 431-4370 • Fax (212) 941-7842

Springer Publishing Company

The Practice of Rational Emotive Behavior Therapy
Second Edition
Albert Ellis, PhD, and Windy Dryden, PhD

This volume systematically reviews the practice of Rational Emotive Behavior Therapy and shows how it can be used by therapists in a variety of clinical settings. The book begins with an explanation of REBT as a general treatment model. It then addresses different treatment modalities, including individual, couple, family, and sex therapy.

The new edition modernizes the pioneering theories of Albert Ellis and contains a complete updating of references over the past ten years. The authors have added new information on teaching the principles of unconditional self-acceptance in a structured, group setting. With extensive use of actual case examples to illustrate each of the different settings, this volume will appeal to clinical and counseling psychologists as well as any other helping professionals involved in therapy.

Contents:

The General Theory of REBT • The Basic Practice of REBT • A Case Illustration of the Basic Practice of REBT: The Case of Jane • Individual Therapy • Couples Therapy • Family Therapy • Group Therapy • Rational Emotive Behavior Marathons and Intensives • Teaching the Principles of Unconditioned Self-Acceptance in a Structured Group Setting • The Rational Emotive Behavioral Approach to Sex Therapy • The Use of Hypnosis with REBT • How to Maintain and Enhance Your Rational Emotive Behavior Therapy Gains

1997 280pp 0-8261-5471-9 hardcover

536 Broadway, New York, NY 10012-3955 • (212) 431-4370 • Fax (212) 941-7842